# TREES

OF

# MISSOURI

## IDENTIFICATION
## RECORD BOOK

Dr. Moss

## Your Feedback is Appreciated!!!

Please consider leaving us "5 Stars" on your Amazon review.

Thank you!

## This Tree Identification Record Book
### Belongs To:

_____

There are approximately over 100 tree species found in the state of Missouri! With an estimated 8 billion live trees growing in Missouri forests, it equates to approximately one-third of forested land - that's 15 million acres of forests. The most common three species are oaks, walnuts and red cedars. Fun fact: Almost all of Missouri was once covered with forests.

Use this record book to identify and record the many types of trees you come across!

## Environment

**Location / GPS:** _____ **Date** _____

**Season:** ○ Spring  ○ Summer  ○ Fall  ○ Winter

**Surroundings:** ○ Hedgerows  ○ Field  ○ Park  ○ Woodland  ○ Water
○ Other _____

**Setting:** ○ Natural  ○ Artificial  **Type:** ○ Evergreen  ○ Deciduous

**Notes:** _____
_____

## General

**Shape:** ○ Vase  ○ Columnar  ○ Round  ○ (Other) _____

**Features:** ○ Conical/Spire  ○ Spreading  ○ Upright  ○ Weeping
○ (Other) _____

**Branching:** ○ Opposite  ○ Alternate  **Estimated Age:** _____

**Notes:** _____
_____

## Needles or Leaves

**Type:** ○ Needle  ○ Simple Broadleaf  ○ Compound Broadleaf  ○ Scales

**Shape:** ○ Cordate (heart-shaped)  ○ Lanceolate (long and narrow)
○ Deltoid (triangular)  ○ Obicular (round)  ○ Ovate (egg-shaped)
○ Palm and Maple  ○ Lobed

**Structure:** ○ Simple (attached to twigs or twig stems)
○ Compound (attached to single lead steam)

**Notes:** _____
_____

## Flowers, Fruits & Seeds

**Flower Type:** ○ Single Blooms  ○ Clustered Blooms  ○ Catkins

**Fruits / Seeds:** ○ Berries  ○ Apples  ○ Pears  ○ Nuts  ○ Acorns
○ Cones  ○ Capsules  ○ Catkins  ○ (Other) _____

**Notes:** _____
_____

## Leaf Buds & Twigs

**Bud Type:** ○ Terminal (grows at tip of a shoot causing shoot to grow longer)
○ Lateral (grow along sides of a shoot causing sideways growth)

**Twig Features:** ○ Smooth  ○ Hairy  ○ Spines  ○ Corky Ribs
○ (Other) _____

**Notes:** _____

## Bark

**Texture:** ○ Furrowed  ○ Scaly  ○ Peeling  ○ Smooth  ○ Shiny
○ Fissured  ○ Ridges / Depressions  ○ Papery  ○ Warty
○ (Other) _____

**Color:** ○ Gray  ○ Brown  ○ Cinnamon  ○ White  ○ Silver
○ Green  ○ Copper  ○ (Other) _____

**Notes:** _____

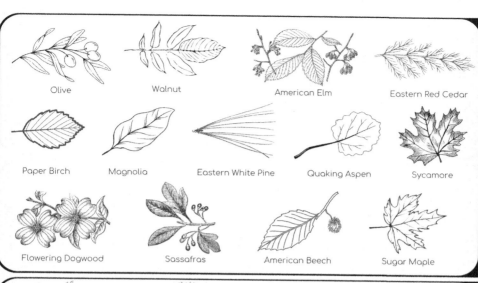

Olive · Walnut · American Elm · Eastern Red Cedar

Paper Birch · Magnolia · Eastern White Pine · Quaking Aspen · Sycamore

Flowering Dogwood · Sassafras · American Beech · Sugar Maple

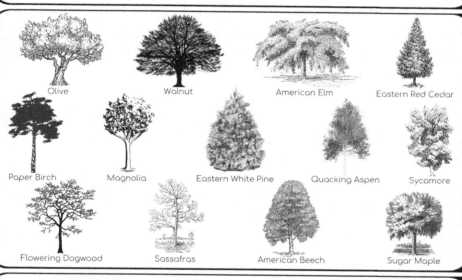

Olive · Walnut · American Elm · Eastern Red Cedar

Paper Birch · Magnolia · Eastern White Pine · Quacking Aspen · Sycamore

Flowering Dogwood · Sassafras · American Beech · Sugar Maple

## Environment

Location / GPS: _____ Date _____

Season: ○ Spring ○ Summer ○ Fall ○ Winter

Surroundings: ○ Hedgerows ○ Field ○ Park ○ Woodland ○ Water
○ Other _____

Setting: ○ Natural ○ Artificial     Type: ○ Evergreen ○ Deciduous

Notes: _____
_____

## General

Shape: ○ Vase ○ Columnar ○ Round ○ (Other) _____

Features: ○ Conical/Spire ○ Spreading ○ Upright ○ Weeping
○ (Other) _____

Branching: ○ Opposite ○ Alternate     Estimated Age: _____

Notes: _____
_____

## Needles or Leaves

Type: ○ Needle ○ Simple Broadleaf ○ Compound Broadleaf ○ Scales

Shape: ○ Cordate (heart-shaped) ○ Lanceolate (long and narrow)
○ Deltoid (triangular) ○ Obicular (round) ○ Ovate (egg-shaped)
○ Palm and Maple ○ Lobed

Structure: ○ Simple (attached to twigs or twig stems)
○ Compound (attached to single lead steam)

Notes: _____
_____

## Flowers, Fruits & Seeds

Flower Type: ○ Single Blooms ○ Clustered Blooms ○ Catkins

Fruits / Seeds: ○ Berries ○ Apples ○ Pears ○ Nuts ○ Acorns
○ Cones ○ Capsules ○ Catkins ○ (Other) _____

Notes: _____
_____

## Leaf Buds & Twigs

Bud Type: ○ Terminal (grows at tip of a shoot causing shoot to grow longer)
○ Lateral (grow along sides of a shoot causing sideways growth)

Twig Features: ○ Smooth ○ Hairy ○ Spines ○ Corky Ribs
○ (Other) _____

Notes: _____

## Bark

Texture: ○ Furrowed ○ Scaly ○ Peeling ○ Smooth ○ Shiny
○ Fissured ○ Ridges / Depressions ○ Papery ○ Warty
○ (Other) _____

Color: ○ Gray ○ Brown ○ Cinnamon ○ White ○ Silver
○ Green ○ Copper ○ (Other) _____

Notes: _____

## Common Leafs

Olive

Walnut

American Elm

Eastern Red Cedar

Paper Birch

Magnolia

Eastern White Pine

Quaking Aspen

Sycamore

Flowering Dogwood

Sassafras

American Beech

Sugar Maple

## Common Trees

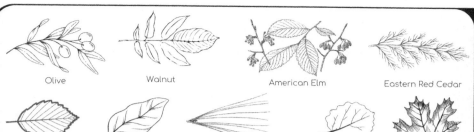
Olive

Walnut

American Elm

Eastern Red Cedar

Paper Birch

Magnolia

Eastern White Pine

Quacking Aspen

Sycamore

Flowering Dogwood

Sassafras

American Beech

Sugar Maple

## Additional Notes

## Environment

Location / GPS: _____  Date _____

Season: ◯ Spring  ◯ Summer  ◯ Fall  ◯ Winter

Surroundings: ◯ Hedgerows  ◯ Field  ◯ Park  ◯ Woodland  ◯ Water
◯ Other _____

Setting: ◯ Natural  ◯ Artificial    Type: ◯ Evergreen  ◯ Deciduous

Notes: _____
_____

## General

Shape: ◯ Vase  ◯ Columnar  ◯ Round  ◯ (Other) _____

Features: ◯ Conical/Spire  ◯ Spreading  ◯ Upright  ◯ Weeping
◯ (Other) _____

Branching: ◯ Opposite  ◯ Alternate    Estimated Age: _____

Notes: _____
_____

## Needles or Leaves

Type: ◯ Needle  ◯ Simple Broadleaf  ◯ Compound Broadleaf  ◯ Scales

Shape: ◯ Cordate (heart-shaped)  ◯ Lanceolate (long and narrow)
◯ Deltoid (triangular)  ◯ Obicular (round)  ◯ Ovate (egg-shaped)
◯ Palm and Maple  ◯ Lobed

Structure: ◯ Simple (attached to twigs or twig stems)
◯ Compound (attached to single lead steam)

Notes: _____
_____

## Flowers, Fruits & Seeds

Flower Type: ◯ Single Blooms  ◯ Clustered Blooms  ◯ Catkins

Fruits / Seeds: ◯ Berries  ◯ Apples  ◯ Pears  ◯ Nuts  ◯ Acorns
◯ Cones  ◯ Capsules  ◯ Catkins  ◯ (Other) _____

Notes: _____
_____

## Leaf Buds & Twigs

Bud Type: ◯ Terminal (grows at tip of a shoot causing shoot to grow longer)
◯ Lateral (grow along sides of a shoot causing sideways growth)

Twig Features: ◯ Smooth  ◯ Hairy  ◯ Spines  ◯ Corky Ribs
◯ (Other) _____

Notes: _____

## Bark

Texture: ◯ Furrowed  ◯ Scaly  ◯ Peeling  ◯ Smooth  ◯ Shiny
◯ Fissured  ◯ Ridges / Depressions  ◯ Papery  ◯ Warty
◯ (Other) _____

Color: ◯ Gray  ◯ Brown  ◯ Cinnamon  ◯ White  ◯ Silver
◯ Green  ◯ Copper  ◯ (Other) _____

Notes: _____

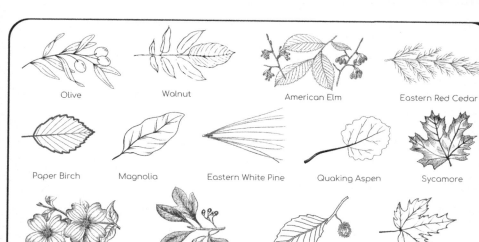

Olive

Walnut

American Elm

Eastern Red Cedar

Paper Birch

Magnolia

Eastern White Pine

Quaking Aspen

Sycamore

Flowering Dogwood

Sassafras

American Beech

Sugar Maple

Olive

Walnut

American Elm

Eastern Red Cedar

Paper Birch

Magnolia

Eastern White Pine

Quacking Aspen

Sycamore

Flowering Dogwood

Sassafras

American Beech

Sugar Maple

## Environment

Location / GPS: _____ Date _____

Season: ○ Spring ○ Summer ○ Fall ○ Winter

Surroundings: ○ Hedgerows ○ Field ○ Park ○ Woodland ○ Water
○ Other _____

Setting: ○ Natural ○ Artificial    Type: ○ Evergreen ○ Deciduous

Notes: _____
_____

## General

Shape: ○ Vase ○ Columnar ○ Round ○ (Other) _____

Features: ○ Conical/Spire ○ Spreading ○ Upright ○ Weeping
○ (Other) _____

Branching: ○ Opposite ○ Alternate    Estimated Age: _____

Notes: _____
_____

## Needles or Leaves

Type: ○ Needle ○ Simple Broadleaf ○ Compound Broadleaf ○ Scales

Shape: ○ Cordate (heart-shaped) ○ Lanceolate (long and narrow)
○ Deltoid (triangular) ○ Obicular (round) ○ Ovate (egg-shaped)
○ Palm and Maple ○ Lobed

Structure: ○ Simple (attached to twigs or twig stems)
○ Compound (attached to single lead steam)

Notes: _____
_____

## Flowers, Fruits & Seeds

Flower Type: ○ Single Blooms ○ Clustered Blooms ○ Catkins

Fruits / Seeds: ○ Berries ○ Apples ○ Pears ○ Nuts ○ Acorns
○ Cones ○ Capsules ○ Catkins ○ (Other) _____

Notes: _____
_____

## Leaf Buds & Twigs

Bud Type: ○ Terminal (grows at tip of a shoot causing shoot to grow longer)
○ Lateral (grow along sides of a shoot causing sideways growth)

Twig Features: ○ Smooth ○ Hairy ○ Spines ○ Corky Ribs
○ (Other) _____

Notes: _____

## Bark

Texture: ○ Furrowed ○ Scaly ○ Peeling ○ Smooth ○ Shiny
○ Fissured ○ Ridges / Depressions ○ Papery ○ Warty
○ (Other) _____

Color: ○ Gray ○ Brown ○ Cinnamon ○ White ○ Silver
○ Green ○ Copper ○ (Other) _____

Notes: _____

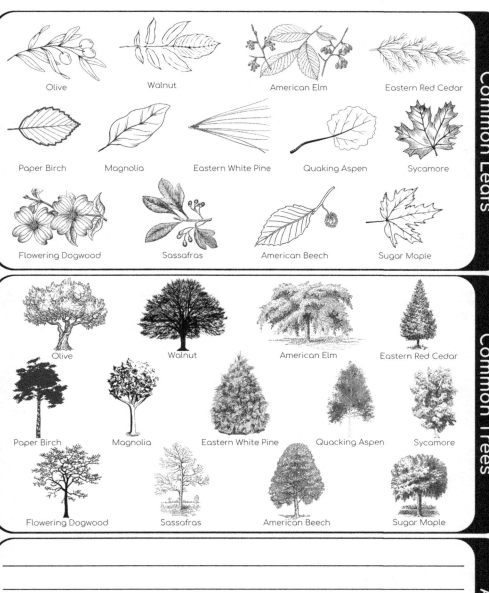

Olive
Walnut
American Elm
Eastern Red Cedar

Paper Birch
Magnolia
Eastern White Pine
Quaking Aspen
Sycamore

Flowering Dogwood
Sassafras
American Beech
Sugar Maple

Olive
Walnut
American Elm
Eastern Red Cedar

Paper Birch
Magnolia
Eastern White Pine
Quacking Aspen
Sycamore

Flowering Dogwood
Sassafras
American Beech
Sugar Maple

## Environment

Location / GPS: _____ Date _____

Season: ○ Spring ○ Summer ○ Fall ○ Winter

Surroundings: ○ Hedgerows ○ Field ○ Park ○ Woodland ○ Water
○ Other_____

Setting: ○ Natural ○ Artificial  Type: ○ Evergreen ○ Deciduous

Notes: _____
_____

## General

Shape: ○ Vase ○ Columnar ○ Round ○ (Other) _____

Features: ○ Conical/Spire ○ Spreading ○ Upright ○ Weeping
○ (Other) _____

Branching: ○ Opposite ○ Alternate  Estimated Age: _____

Notes: _____
_____

## Needles or Leaves

Type: ○ Needle ○ Simple Broadleaf ○ Compound Broadleaf ○ Scales

Shape: ○ Cordate (heart-shaped) ○ Lanceolate (long and narrow)
○ Deltoid (triangular) ○ Obicular (round) ○ Ovate (egg-shaped)
○ Palm and Maple ○ Lobed

Structure: ○ Simple (attached to twigs or twig stems)
○ Compound (attached to single lead steam)

Notes: _____
_____

## Flowers, Fruits & Seeds

Flower Type: ○ Single Blooms ○ Clustered Blooms ○ Catkins

Fruits / Seeds: ○ Berries ○ Apples ○ Pears ○ Nuts ○ Acorns
○ Cones ○ Capsules ○ Catkins ○ (Other) _____

Notes: _____
_____

## Leaf Buds & Twigs

Bud Type: ○ Terminal (grows at tip of a shoot causing shoot to grow longer)
○ Lateral (grow along sides of a shoot causing sideways growth)

Twig Features: ○ Smooth ○ Hairy ○ Spines ○ Corky Ribs
○ (Other) _____

Notes: _____

## Bark

Texture: ○ Furrowed ○ Scaly ○ Peeling ○ Smooth ○ Shiny
○ Fissured ○ Ridges / Depressions ○ Papery ○ Warty
○ (Other) _____

Color: ○ Gray ○ Brown ○ Cinnamon ○ White ○ Silver
○ Green ○ Copper ○ (Other) _____

Notes: _____

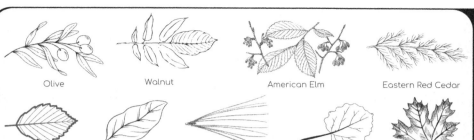

Olive

Walnut

American Elm

Eastern Red Cedar

Paper Birch

Magnolia

Eastern White Pine

Quaking Aspen

Sycamore

Flowering Dogwood

Sassafras

American Beech

Sugar Maple

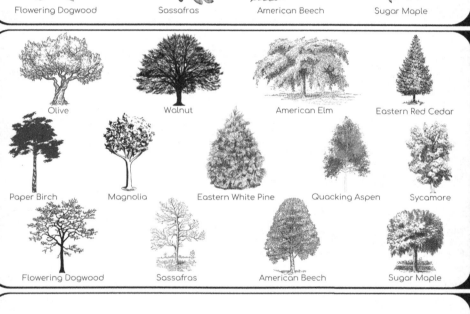

Olive

Walnut

American Elm

Eastern Red Cedar

Paper Birch

Magnolia

Eastern White Pine

Quacking Aspen

Sycamore

Flowering Dogwood

Sassafras

American Beech

Sugar Maple

## Environment

Location / GPS: _____ Date _____

Season: ○ Spring ○ Summer ○ Fall ○ Winter

Surroundings: ○ Hedgerows ○ Field ○ Park ○ Woodland ○ Water
○ Other _____

Setting: ○ Natural ○ Artificial Type: ○ Evergreen ○ Deciduous

Notes: _____
_____

## General

Shape: ○ Vase ○ Columnar ○ Round ○ (Other) _____

Features: ○ Conical/Spire ○ Spreading ○ Upright ○ Weeping
○ (Other) _____

Branching: ○ Opposite ○ Alternate Estimated Age: _____

Notes: _____
_____

## Needles or Leaves

Type: ○ Needle ○ Simple Broadleaf ○ Compound Broadleaf ○ Scales

Shape: ○ Cordate (heart-shaped) ○ Lanceolate (long and narrow)
○ Deltoid (triangular) ○ Obicular (round) ○ Ovate (egg-shaped)
○ Palm and Maple ○ Lobed

Structure: ○ Simple (attached to twigs or twig stems)
○ Compound (attached to single lead steam)

Notes: _____
_____

## Flowers, Fruits & Seeds

Flower Type: ○ Single Blooms ○ Clustered Blooms ○ Catkins

Fruits / Seeds: ○ Berries ○ Apples ○ Pears ○ Nuts ○ Acorns
○ Cones ○ Capsules ○ Catkins ○ (Other) _____

Notes: _____
_____

## Leaf Buds & Twigs

Bud Type: ○ Terminal (grows at tip of a shoot causing shoot to grow longer)
○ Lateral (grow along sides of a shoot causing sideways growth)

Twig Features: ○ Smooth ○ Hairy ○ Spines ○ Corky Ribs
○ (Other) _____

Notes: _____

## Bark

Texture: ○ Furrowed ○ Scaly ○ Peeling ○ Smooth ○ Shiny
○ Fissured ○ Ridges / Depressions ○ Papery ○ Warty
○ (Other) _____

Color: ○ Gray ○ Brown ○ Cinnamon ○ White ○ Silver
○ Green ○ Copper ○ (Other) _____

Notes: _____

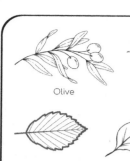
Olive

Walnut

American Elm

Eastern Red Cedar

Paper Birch

Magnolia

Eastern White Pine

Quaking Aspen

Sycamore

Flowering Dogwood

Sassafras

American Beech

Sugar Maple

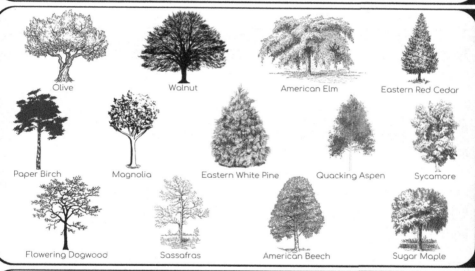

Olive

Walnut

American Elm

Eastern Red Cedar

Paper Birch

Magnolia

Eastern White Pine

Quacking Aspen

Sycamore

Flowering Dogwood

Sassafras

American Beech

Sugar Maple

## Environment

Location / GPS: _____ Date _____

Season: ○ Spring ○ Summer ○ Fall ○ Winter

Surroundings: ○ Hedgerows ○ Field ○ Park ○ Woodland ○ Water
○ Other _____

Setting: ○ Natural ○ Artificial **Type:** ○ Evergreen ○ Deciduous

Notes: _____
_____

## General

Shape: ○ Vase ○ Columnar ○ Round ○ (Other) _____

Features: ○ Conical/Spire ○ Spreading ○ Upright ○ Weeping
○ (Other) _____

Branching: ○ Opposite ○ Alternate **Estimated Age:** _____

Notes: _____
_____

## Needles or Leaves

Type: ○ Needle ○ Simple Broadleaf ○ Compound Broadleaf ○ Scales

Shape: ○ Cordate (heart-shaped) ○ Lanceolate (long and narrow)
○ Deltoid (triangular) ○ Obicular (round) ○ Ovate (egg-shaped)
○ Palm and Maple ○ Lobed

Structure: ○ Simple (attached to twigs or twig stems)
○ Compound (attached to single lead steam)

Notes: _____
_____

## Flowers, Fruits & Seeds

Flower Type: ○ Single Blooms ○ Clustered Blooms ○ Catkins

Fruits / Seeds: ○ Berries ○ Apples ○ Pears ○ Nuts ○ Acorns
○ Cones ○ Capsules ○ Catkins ○ (Other) _____

Notes: _____
_____

## Leaf Buds & Twigs

Bud Type: ○ Terminal (grows at tip of a shoot causing shoot to grow longer)
○ Lateral (grow along sides of a shoot causing sideways growth)

Twig Features: ○ Smooth ○ Hairy ○ Spines ○ Corky Ribs
○ (Other) _____

Notes: _____

## Bark

Texture: ○ Furrowed ○ Scaly ○ Peeling ○ Smooth ○ Shiny
○ Fissured ○ Ridges / Depressions ○ Papery ○ Warty
○ (Other) _____

Color: ○ Gray ○ Brown ○ Cinnamon ○ White ○ Silver
○ Green ○ Copper ○ (Other) _____

Notes: _____

Olive

Walnut

American Elm

Eastern Red Cedar

Paper Birch

Magnolia

Eastern White Pine

Quaking Aspen

Sycamore

Flowering Dogwood

Sassafras

American Beech

Sugar Maple

Olive

Walnut

American Elm

Eastern Red Cedar

Paper Birch

Magnolia

Eastern White Pine

Quacking Aspen

Sycamore

Flowering Dogwood

Sassafras

American Beech

Sugar Maple

## Environment

Location / GPS: _____ Date _____

Season: ○ Spring  ○ Summer  ○ Fall  ○ Winter

Surroundings: ○ Hedgerows  ○ Field  ○ Park  ○ Woodland  ○ Water
○ Other_____

Setting: ○ Natural  ○ Artificial    Type: ○ Evergreen  ○ Deciduous

Notes: _____
_____

## General

Shape: ○ Vase  ○ Columnar  ○ Round  ○ (Other) _____

Features: ○ Conical/Spire  ○ Spreading  ○ Upright  ○ Weeping
○ (Other) _____

Branching: ○ Opposite  ○ Alternate    Estimated Age: _____

Notes: _____
_____

## Needles or Leaves

Type: ○ Needle  ○ Simple Broadleaf  ○ Compound Broadleaf  ○ Scales

Shape: ○ Cordate (heart-shaped)  ○ Lanceolate (long and narrow)
○ Deltoid (triangular)  ○ Obicular (round)  ○ Ovate (egg-shaped)
○ Palm and Maple  ○ Lobed

Structure: ○ Simple (attached to twigs or twig stems)
○ Compound (attached to single lead steam)

Notes: _____
_____

## Flowers, Fruits & Seeds

Flower Type: ○ Single Blooms  ○ Clustered Blooms  ○ Catkins

Fruits / Seeds: ○ Berries  ○ Apples  ○ Pears  ○ Nuts  ○ Acorns
○ Cones  ○ Capsules  ○ Catkins  ○ (Other) _____

Notes: _____
_____

## Leaf Buds & Twigs

Bud Type: ○ Terminal (grows at tip of a shoot causing shoot to grow longer)
○ Lateral (grow along sides of a shoot causing sideways growth)

Twig Features: ○ Smooth  ○ Hairy  ○ Spines  ○ Corky Ribs
○ (Other) _____

Notes: _____

## Bark

Texture: ○ Furrowed  ○ Scaly  ○ Peeling  ○ Smooth  ○ Shiny
○ Fissured  ○ Ridges / Depressions  ○ Papery  ○ Warty
○ (Other) _____

Color: ○ Gray  ○ Brown  ○ Cinnamon  ○ White  ○ Silver
○ Green  ○ Copper  ○ (Other) _____

Notes: _____

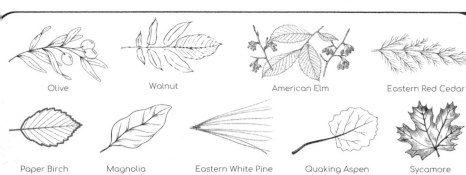

Olive

Walnut

American Elm

Eastern Red Cedar

Paper Birch

Magnolia

Eastern White Pine

Quaking Aspen

Sycamore

Flowering Dogwood

Sassafras

American Beech

Sugar Maple

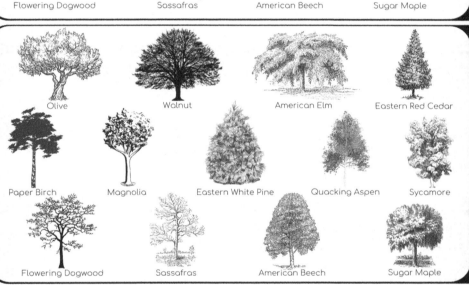

Olive

Walnut

American Elm

Eastern Red Cedar

Paper Birch

Magnolia

Eastern White Pine

Quacking Aspen

Sycamore

Flowering Dogwood

Sassafras

American Beech

Sugar Maple

## Environment

Location / GPS: _____ Date _____

Season: ○ Spring ○ Summer ○ Fall ○ Winter

Surroundings: ○ Hedgerows ○ Field ○ Park ○ Woodland ○ Water
○ Other _____

Setting: ○ Natural ○ Artificial    Type: ○ Evergreen ○ Deciduous

Notes: _____
_____

## General

Shape: ○ Vase ○ Columnar ○ Round ○ (Other) _____

Features: ○ Conical/Spire ○ Spreading ○ Upright ○ Weeping
○ (Other) _____

Branching: ○ Opposite ○ Alternate    Estimated Age: _____

Notes: _____
_____

## Needles or Leaves

Type: ○ Needle ○ Simple Broadleaf ○ Compound Broadleaf ○ Scales

Shape: ○ Cordate (heart-shaped) ○ Lanceolate (long and narrow)
○ Deltoid (triangular) ○ Obicular (round) ○ Ovate (egg-shaped)
○ Palm and Maple ○ Lobed

Structure: ○ Simple (attached to twigs or twig stems)
○ Compound (attached to single lead steam)

Notes: _____
_____

## Flowers, Fruits & Seeds

Flower Type: ○ Single Blooms ○ Clustered Blooms ○ Catkins

Fruits / Seeds: ○ Berries ○ Apples ○ Pears ○ Nuts ○ Acorns
○ Cones ○ Capsules ○ Catkins ○ (Other) _____

Notes: _____
_____

## Leaf Buds & Twigs

Bud Type: ○ Terminal (grows at tip of a shoot causing shoot to grow longer)
○ Lateral (grow along sides of a shoot causing sideways growth)

Twig Features: ○ Smooth ○ Hairy ○ Spines ○ Corky Ribs
○ (Other) _____

Notes: _____

## Bark

Texture: ○ Furrowed ○ Scaly ○ Peeling ○ Smooth ○ Shiny
○ Fissured ○ Ridges / Depressions ○ Papery ○ Warty
○ (Other) _____

Color: ○ Gray ○ Brown ○ Cinnamon ○ White ○ Silver
○ Green ○ Copper ○ (Other) _____

Notes: _____

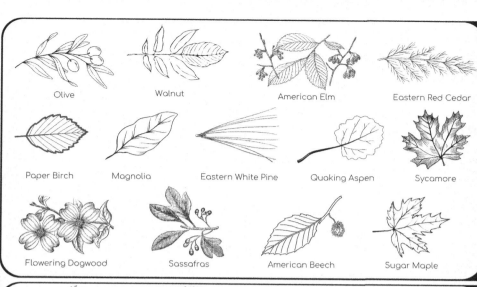

Olive  Walnut  American Elm  Eastern Red Cedar

Paper Birch  Magnolia  Eastern White Pine  Quaking Aspen  Sycamore

Flowering Dogwood  Sassafras  American Beech  Sugar Maple

Olive  Walnut  American Elm  Eastern Red Cedar

Paper Birch  Magnolia  Eastern White Pine  Quacking Aspen  Sycamore

Flowering Dogwood  Sassafras  American Beech  Sugar Maple

## Environment

Location / GPS: _____ Date _____

Season: ○ Spring ○ Summer ○ Fall ○ Winter

Surroundings: ○ Hedgerows ○ Field ○ Park ○ Woodland ○ Water
○ Other _____

Setting: ○ Natural ○ Artificial    Type: ○ Evergreen ○ Deciduous

Notes: _____
_____

## General

Shape: ○ Vase ○ Columnar ○ Round ○ (Other) _____

Features: ○ Conical/Spire ○ Spreading ○ Upright ○ Weeping
○ (Other) _____

Branching: ○ Opposite ○ Alternate    Estimated Age: _____

Notes: _____
_____

## Needles or Leaves

Type: ○ Needle ○ Simple Broadleaf ○ Compound Broadleaf ○ Scales

Shape: ○ Cordate (heart-shaped) ○ Lanceolate (long and narrow)
○ Deltoid (triangular) ○ Obicular (round) ○ Ovate (egg-shaped)
○ Palm and Maple ○ Lobed

Structure: ○ Simple (attached to twigs or twig stems)
○ Compound (attached to single lead steam)

Notes: _____
_____

## Flowers, Fruits & Seeds

Flower Type: ○ Single Blooms ○ Clustered Blooms ○ Catkins

Fruits / Seeds: ○ Berries ○ Apples ○ Pears ○ Nuts ○ Acorns
○ Cones ○ Capsules ○ Catkins ○ (Other) _____

Notes: _____
_____

## Leaf Buds & Twigs

Bud Type: ○ Terminal (grows at tip of a shoot causing shoot to grow longer)
○ Lateral (grow along sides of a shoot causing sideways growth)

Twig Features: ○ Smooth ○ Hairy ○ Spines ○ Corky Ribs
○ (Other) _____

Notes: _____

## Bark

Texture: ○ Furrowed ○ Scaly ○ Peeling ○ Smooth ○ Shiny
○ Fissured ○ Ridges / Depressions ○ Papery ○ Warty
○ (Other) _____

Color: ○ Gray ○ Brown ○ Cinnamon ○ White ○ Silver
○ Green ○ Copper ○ (Other) _____

Notes: _____

Olive

Walnut

American Elm

Eastern Red Cedar

Paper Birch

Magnolia

Eastern White Pine

Quaking Aspen

Sycamore

Flowering Dogwood

Sassafras

American Beech

Sugar Maple

Olive

Walnut

American Elm

Eastern Red Cedar

Paper Birch

Magnolia

Eastern White Pine

Quacking Aspen

Sycamore

Flowering Dogwood

Sassafras

American Beech

Sugar Maple

## Environment

Location / GPS: _____  Date _____

Season: ⚪ Spring ⚪ Summer ⚪ Fall ⚪ Winter

Surroundings: ⚪ Hedgerows ⚪ Field ⚪ Park ⚪ Woodland ⚪ Water
⚪ Other_____

Setting: ⚪ Natural ⚪ Artificial  Type: ⚪ Evergreen ⚪ Deciduous

Notes: _____
_____

## General

Shape: ⚪ Vase ⚪ Columnar ⚪ Round ⚪ (Other) _____

Features: ⚪ Conical/Spire ⚪ Spreading ⚪ Upright ⚪ Weeping
⚪ (Other) _____

Branching: ⚪ Opposite ⚪ Alternate  Estimated Age: _____

Notes: _____
_____

## Needles or Leaves

Type: ⚪ Needle ⚪ Simple Broadleaf ⚪ Compound Broadleaf ⚪ Scales

Shape: ⚪ Cordate (heart-shaped) ⚪ Lanceolate (long and narrow)
⚪ Deltoid (triangular) ⚪ Obicular (round) ⚪ Ovate (egg-shaped)
⚪ Palm and Maple ⚪ Lobed

Structure: ⚪ Simple (attached to twigs or twig stems)
⚪ Compound (attached to single lead steam)

Notes: _____
_____

## Flowers, Fruits & Seeds

Flower Type: ⚪ Single Blooms ⚪ Clustered Blooms ⚪ Catkins

Fruits / Seeds: ⚪ Berries ⚪ Apples ⚪ Pears ⚪ Nuts ⚪ Acorns
⚪ Cones ⚪ Capsules ⚪ Catkins ⚪ (Other) _____

Notes: _____
_____

## Leaf Buds & Twigs

Bud Type: ⚪ Terminal (grows at tip of a shoot causing shoot to grow longer)
⚪ Lateral (grow along sides of a shoot causing sideways growth)

Twig Features: ⚪ Smooth ⚪ Hairy ⚪ Spines ⚪ Corky Ribs
⚪ (Other) _____

Notes: _____

## Bark

Texture: ⚪ Furrowed ⚪ Scaly ⚪ Peeling ⚪ Smooth ⚪ Shiny
⚪ Fissured ⚪ Ridges / Depressions ⚪ Papery ⚪ Warty
⚪ (Other) _____

Color: ⚪ Gray ⚪ Brown ⚪ Cinnamon ⚪ White ⚪ Silver
⚪ Green ⚪ Copper ⚪ (Other) _____

Notes: _____

Olive

Walnut

American Elm

Eastern Red Cedar

Paper Birch

Magnolia

Eastern White Pine

Quaking Aspen

Sycamore

Flowering Dogwood

Sassafras

American Beech

Sugar Maple

Olive

Walnut

American Elm

Eastern Red Cedar

Paper Birch

Magnolia

Eastern White Pine

Quacking Aspen

Sycamore

Flowering Dogwood

Sassafras

American Beech

Sugar Maple

## Environment

Location / GPS: _____ Date _____|_____

Season: ○ Spring ○ Summer ○ Fall ○ Winter

Surroundings: ○ Hedgerows ○ Field ○ Park ○ Woodland ○ Water
○ Other_____

Setting: ○ Natural ○ Artificial   Type: ○ Evergreen ○ Deciduous

Notes: _____
_____
_____

## General

Shape: ○ Vase ○ Columnar ○ Round ○ (Other) _____

Features: ○ Conical/Spire ○ Spreading ○ Upright ○ Weeping
○ (Other) _____

Branching: ○ Opposite ○ Alternate   Estimated Age: _____

Notes: _____
_____
_____

## Needles or Leaves

Type: ○ Needle ○ Simple Broadleaf ○ Compound Broadleaf ○ Scales

Shape: ○ Cordate (heart-shaped) ○ Lanceolate (long and narrow)
○ Deltoid (triangular) ○ Obicular (round) ○ Ovate (egg-shaped)
○ Palm and Maple ○ Lobed

Structure: ○ Simple (attached to twigs or twig stems)
○ Compound (attached to single lead steam)

Notes: _____
_____
_____

## Flowers, Fruits & Seeds

Flower Type: ○ Single Blooms ○ Clustered Blooms ○ Catkins

Fruits / Seeds: ○ Berries ○ Apples ○ Pears ○ Nuts ○ Acorns
○ Cones ○ Capsules ○ Catkins ○ (Other) _____

Notes: _____
_____
_____

## Leaf Buds & Twigs

Bud Type: ○ Terminal (grows at tip of a shoot causing shoot to grow longer)
○ Lateral (grow along sides of a shoot causing sideways growth)

Twig Features: ○ Smooth ○ Hairy ○ Spines ○ Corky Ribs
○ (Other) _____

Notes: _____
_____

## Bark

Texture: ○ Furrowed ○ Scaly ○ Peeling ○ Smooth ○ Shiny
○ Fissured ○ Ridges / Depressions ○ Papery ○ Warty
○ (Other) _____

Color: ○ Gray ○ Brown ○ Cinnamon ○ White ○ Silver
○ Green ○ Copper ○ (Other) _____

Notes: _____

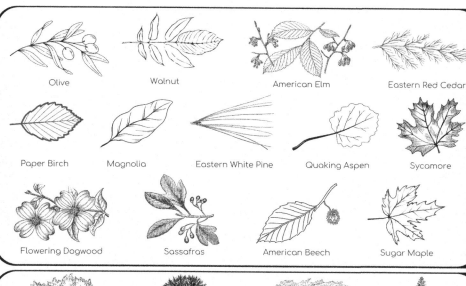

Olive | Walnut | American Elm | Eastern Red Cedar

Paper Birch | Magnolia | Eastern White Pine | Quaking Aspen | Sycamore

Flowering Dogwood | Sassafras | American Beech | Sugar Maple

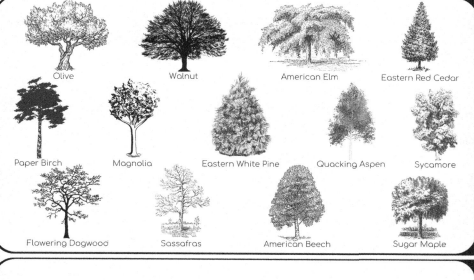

Olive | Walnut | American Elm | Eastern Red Cedar

Paper Birch | Magnolia | Eastern White Pine | Quacking Aspen | Sycamore

Flowering Dogwood | Sassafras | American Beech | Sugar Maple

## Environment

Location / GPS: _____ Date _____

Season: ○ Spring ○ Summer ○ Fall ○ Winter

Surroundings: ○ Hedgerows ○ Field ○ Park ○ Woodland ○ Water
○ Other _____

Setting: ○ Natural ○ Artificial **Type:** ○ Evergreen ○ Deciduous

Notes: _____
_____

## General

Shape: ○ Vase ○ Columnar ○ Round ○ (Other) _____

Features: ○ Conical/Spire ○ Spreading ○ Upright ○ Weeping
○ (Other) _____

Branching: ○ Opposite ○ Alternate **Estimated Age:** _____

Notes: _____
_____

## Needles or Leaves

Type: ○ Needle ○ Simple Broadleaf ○ Compound Broadleaf ○ Scales

Shape: ○ Cordate (heart-shaped) ○ Lanceolate (long and narrow)
○ Deltoid (triangular) ○ Obicular (round) ○ Ovate (egg-shaped)
○ Palm and Maple ○ Lobed

Structure: ○ Simple (attached to twigs or twig stems)
○ Compound (attached to single lead steam)

Notes: _____
_____

## Flowers, Fruits & Seeds

Flower Type: ○ Single Blooms ○ Clustered Blooms ○ Catkins

Fruits / Seeds: ○ Berries ○ Apples ○ Pears ○ Nuts ○ Acorns
○ Cones ○ Capsules ○ Catkins ○ (Other) _____

Notes: _____
_____

## Leaf Buds & Twigs

Bud Type: ○ Terminal (grows at tip of a shoot causing shoot to grow longer)
○ Lateral (grow along sides of a shoot causing sideways growth)

Twig Features: ○ Smooth ○ Hairy ○ Spines ○ Corky Ribs
○ (Other) _____

Notes: _____

## Bark

Texture: ○ Furrowed ○ Scaly ○ Peeling ○ Smooth ○ Shiny
○ Fissured ○ Ridges / Depressions ○ Papery ○ Warty
○ (Other) _____

Color: ○ Gray ○ Brown ○ Cinnamon ○ White ○ Silver
○ Green ○ Copper ○ (Other) _____

Notes: _____

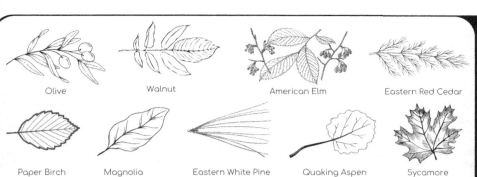

Olive

Walnut

American Elm

Eastern Red Cedar

Paper Birch

Magnolia

Eastern White Pine

Quaking Aspen

Sycamore

Flowering Dogwood

Sassafras

American Beech

Sugar Maple

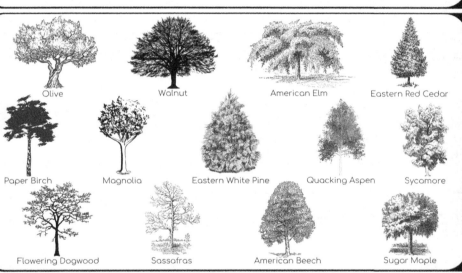

Olive

Walnut

American Elm

Eastern Red Cedar

Paper Birch

Magnolia

Eastern White Pine

Quacking Aspen

Sycamore

Flowering Dogwood

Sassafras

American Beech

Sugar Maple

## Environment

Location / GPS: _____ Date _____

Season: ◯ Spring ◯ Summer ◯ Fall ◯ Winter

Surroundings: ◯ Hedgerows ◯ Field ◯ Park ◯ Woodland ◯ Water
◯ Other _____

Setting: ◯ Natural ◯ Artificial    Type: ◯ Evergreen ◯ Deciduous

Notes: _____
_____

## General

Shape: ◯ Vase ◯ Columnar ◯ Round ◯ (Other) _____

Features: ◯ Conical/Spire ◯ Spreading ◯ Upright ◯ Weeping
◯ (Other) _____

Branching: ◯ Opposite ◯ Alternate    Estimated Age: _____

Notes: _____
_____

## Needles or Leaves

Type: ◯ Needle ◯ Simple Broadleaf ◯ Compound Broadleaf ◯ Scales

Shape: ◯ Cordate (heart-shaped) ◯ Lanceolate (long and narrow)
◯ Deltoid (triangular) ◯ Obicular (round) ◯ Ovate (egg-shaped)
◯ Palm and Maple ◯ Lobed

Structure: ◯ Simple (attached to twigs or twig stems)
◯ Compound (attached to single lead steam)

Notes: _____
_____

## Flowers, Fruits & Seeds

Flower Type: ◯ Single Blooms ◯ Clustered Blooms ◯ Catkins

Fruits / Seeds: ◯ Berries ◯ Apples ◯ Pears ◯ Nuts ◯ Acorns
◯ Cones ◯ Capsules ◯ Catkins ◯ (Other) _____

Notes: _____
_____

## Leaf Buds & Twigs

Bud Type: ◯ Terminal (grows at tip of a shoot causing shoot to grow longer)
◯ Lateral (grow along sides of a shoot causing sideways growth)

Twig Features: ◯ Smooth ◯ Hairy ◯ Spines ◯ Corky Ribs
◯ (Other) _____

Notes: _____

## Bark

Texture: ◯ Furrowed ◯ Scaly ◯ Peeling ◯ Smooth ◯ Shiny
◯ Fissured ◯ Ridges / Depressions ◯ Papery ◯ Warty
◯ (Other) _____

Color: ◯ Gray ◯ Brown ◯ Cinnamon ◯ White ◯ Silver
◯ Green ◯ Copper ◯ (Other) _____

Notes: _____

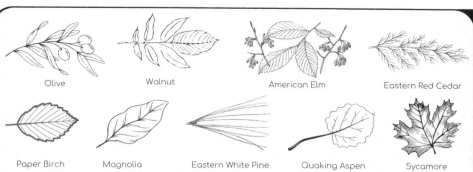

Olive  Walnut  American Elm  Eastern Red Cedar

Paper Birch  Magnolia  Eastern White Pine  Quaking Aspen  Sycamore

Flowering Dogwood  Sassafras  American Beech  Sugar Maple

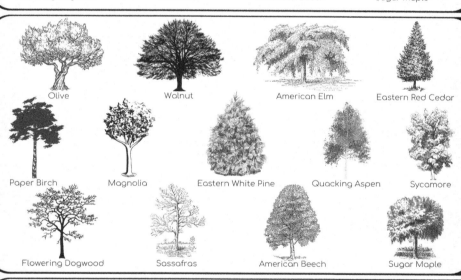

Olive  Walnut  American Elm  Eastern Red Cedar

Paper Birch  Magnolia  Eastern White Pine  Quacking Aspen  Sycamore

Flowering Dogwood  Sassafras  American Beech  Sugar Maple

## Environment

Location / GPS: _____ Date _____

Season: ○ Spring ○ Summer ○ Fall ○ Winter

Surroundings: ○ Hedgerows ○ Field ○ Park ○ Woodland ○ Water
○ Other _____

Setting: ○ Natural ○ Artificial   Type: ○ Evergreen ○ Deciduous

Notes: _____
_____

## General

Shape: ○ Vase ○ Columnar ○ Round ○ (Other) _____

Features: ○ Conical/Spire ○ Spreading ○ Upright ○ Weeping
○ (Other) _____

Branching: ○ Opposite ○ Alternate   Estimated Age: _____

Notes: _____
_____

## Needles or Leaves

Type: ○ Needle ○ Simple Broadleaf ○ Compound Broadleaf ○ Scales

Shape: ○ Cordate (heart-shaped) ○ Lanceolate (long and narrow)
○ Deltoid (triangular) ○ Obicular (round) ○ Ovate (egg-shaped)
○ Palm and Maple ○ Lobed

Structure: ○ Simple (attached to twigs or twig stems)
○ Compound (attached to single lead steam)

Notes: _____
_____

## Flowers, Fruits & Seeds

Flower Type: ○ Single Blooms ○ Clustered Blooms ○ Catkins

Fruits / Seeds: ○ Berries ○ Apples ○ Pears ○ Nuts ○ Acorns
○ Cones ○ Capsules ○ Catkins ○ (Other) _____

Notes: _____
_____

## Leaf Buds & Twigs

Bud Type: ○ Terminal (grows at tip of a shoot causing shoot to grow longer)
○ Lateral (grow along sides of a shoot causing sideways growth)

Twig Features: ○ Smooth ○ Hairy ○ Spines ○ Corky Ribs
○ (Other) _____

Notes: _____

## Bark

Texture: ○ Furrowed ○ Scaly ○ Peeling ○ Smooth ○ Shiny
○ Fissured ○ Ridges / Depressions ○ Papery ○ Warty
○ (Other) _____

Color: ○ Gray ○ Brown ○ Cinnamon ○ White ○ Silver
○ Green ○ Copper ○ (Other) _____

Notes: _____

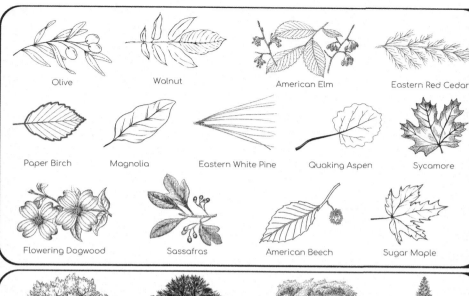

Olive
Walnut
American Elm
Eastern Red Cedar

Paper Birch
Magnolia
Eastern White Pine
Quaking Aspen
Sycamore

Flowering Dogwood
Sassafras
American Beech
Sugar Maple

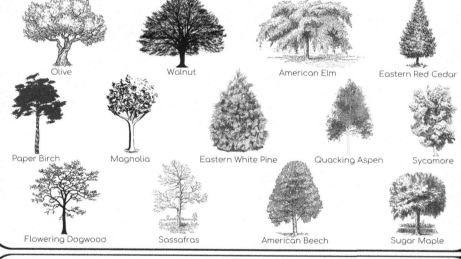

Olive
Walnut
American Elm
Eastern Red Cedar

Paper Birch
Magnolia
Eastern White Pine
Quacking Aspen
Sycamore

Flowering Dogwood
Sassafras
American Beech
Sugar Maple

## Environment

Location / GPS: _____ Date _____

Season: ○ Spring  ○ Summer  ○ Fall  ○ Winter

Surroundings: ○ Hedgerows  ○ Field  ○ Park  ○ Woodland  ○ Water
○ Other _____

Setting: ○ Natural  ○ Artificial    Type: ○ Evergreen  ○ Deciduous

Notes: _____
_____

## General

Shape: ○ Vase  ○ Columnar  ○ Round  ○ (Other) _____

Features: ○ Conical/Spire  ○ Spreading  ○ Upright  ○ Weeping
○ (Other) _____

Branching: ○ Opposite  ○ Alternate    Estimated Age: _____

Notes: _____
_____

## Needles or Leaves

Type: ○ Needle  ○ Simple Broadleaf  ○ Compound Broadleaf  ○ Scales

Shape: ○ Cordate (heart-shaped)  ○ Lanceolate (long and narrow)
○ Deltoid (triangular)  ○ Obicular (round)  ○ Ovate (egg-shaped)
○ Palm and Maple  ○ Lobed

Structure: ○ Simple (attached to twigs or twig stems)
○ Compound (attached to single lead steam)

Notes: _____
_____

## Flowers, Fruits & Seeds

Flower Type: ○ Single Blooms  ○ Clustered Blooms  ○ Catkins

Fruits / Seeds: ○ Berries  ○ Apples  ○ Pears  ○ Nuts  ○ Acorns
○ Cones  ○ Capsules  ○ Catkins  ○ (Other) _____

Notes: _____
_____

## Leaf Buds & Twigs

Bud Type: ○ Terminal (grows at tip of a shoot causing shoot to grow longer)
○ Lateral (grow along sides of a shoot causing sideways growth)

Twig Features: ○ Smooth  ○ Hairy  ○ Spines  ○ Corky Ribs
○ (Other) _____

Notes: _____

## Bark

Texture: ○ Furrowed  ○ Scaly  ○ Peeling  ○ Smooth  ○ Shiny
○ Fissured  ○ Ridges / Depressions  ○ Papery  ○ Warty
○ (Other) _____

Color: ○ Gray  ○ Brown  ○ Cinnamon  ○ White  ○ Silver
○ Green  ○ Copper  ○ (Other) _____

Notes: _____

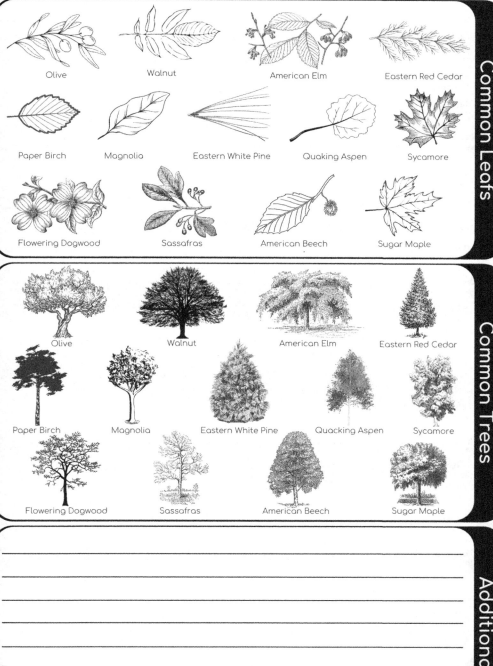

Olive
Walnut
American Elm
Eastern Red Cedar

Paper Birch
Magnolia
Eastern White Pine
Quaking Aspen
Sycamore

Flowering Dogwood
Sassafras
American Beech
Sugar Maple

Olive
Walnut
American Elm
Eastern Red Cedar

Paper Birch
Magnolia
Eastern White Pine
Quacking Aspen
Sycamore

Flowering Dogwood
Sassafras
American Beech
Sugar Maple

## Environment

Location / GPS: _____ Date _____

Season: ○ Spring ○ Summer ○ Fall ○ Winter

Surroundings: ○ Hedgerows ○ Field ○ Park ○ Woodland ○ Water
○ Other _____

Setting: ○ Natural ○ Artificial    Type: ○ Evergreen ○ Deciduous

Notes: _____
_____

## General

Shape: ○ Vase ○ Columnar ○ Round ○ (Other) _____

Features: ○ Conical/Spire ○ Spreading ○ Upright ○ Weeping
○ (Other) _____

Branching: ○ Opposite ○ Alternate    Estimated Age: _____

Notes: _____
_____

## Needles or Leaves

Type: ○ Needle ○ Simple Broadleaf ○ Compound Broadleaf ○ Scales

Shape: ○ Cordate (heart-shaped) ○ Lanceolate (long and narrow)
○ Deltoid (triangular) ○ Obicular (round) ○ Ovate (egg-shaped)
○ Palm and Maple ○ Lobed

Structure: ○ Simple (attached to twigs or twig stems)
○ Compound (attached to single lead steam)

Notes: _____
_____

## Flowers, Fruits & Seeds

Flower Type: ○ Single Blooms ○ Clustered Blooms ○ Catkins

Fruits / Seeds: ○ Berries ○ Apples ○ Pears ○ Nuts ○ Acorns
○ Cones ○ Capsules ○ Catkins ○ (Other) _____

Notes: _____
_____

## Leaf Buds & Twigs

Bud Type: ○ Terminal (grows at tip of a shoot causing shoot to grow longer)
○ Lateral (grow along sides of a shoot causing sideways growth)

Twig Features: ○ Smooth ○ Hairy ○ Spines ○ Corky Ribs
○ (Other) _____

Notes: _____

## Bark

Texture: ○ Furrowed ○ Scaly ○ Peeling ○ Smooth ○ Shiny
○ Fissured ○ Ridges / Depressions ○ Papery ○ Warty
○ (Other) _____

Color: ○ Gray ○ Brown ○ Cinnamon ○ White ○ Silver
○ Green ○ Copper ○ (Other) _____

Notes: _____

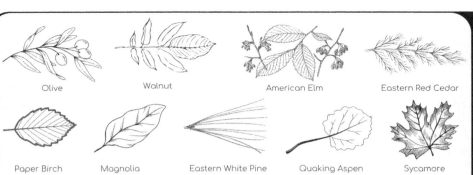

Olive        Walnut        American Elm        Eastern Red Cedar

Paper Birch   Magnolia   Eastern White Pine   Quaking Aspen   Sycamore

Flowering Dogwood   Sassafras   American Beech   Sugar Maple

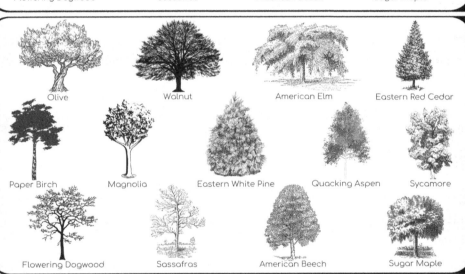

Olive        Walnut        American Elm        Eastern Red Cedar

Paper Birch   Magnolia   Eastern White Pine   Quacking Aspen   Sycamore

Flowering Dogwood   Sassafras   American Beech   Sugar Maple

_____
_____
_____
_____
_____
_____
_____
_____
_____
_____
_____

## Environment

Location / GPS: _____  Date _____

Season:  ○ Spring   ○ Summer   ○ Fall   ○ Winter

Surroundings:  ○ Hedgerows   ○ Field   ○ Park   ○ Woodland   ○ Water
○ Other_____

Setting:  ○ Natural   ○ Artificial   **Type:**  ○ Evergreen   ○ Deciduous

Notes: _____
_____

## General

Shape:  ○ Vase   ○ Columnar   ○ Round   ○(Other) _____

Features:  ○ Conical/Spire   ○ Spreading   ○ Upright   ○ Weeping
○(Other) _____

Branching:  ○ Opposite   ○ Alternate   **Estimated Age:** _____

Notes: _____
_____

## Needles or Leaves

Type:  ○ Needle   ○ Simple Broadleaf   ○ Compound Broadleaf   ○ Scales

Shape:  ○ Cordate (heart-shaped)   ○ Lanceolate (long and narrow)
○ Deltoid (triangular)   ○ Obicular (round)   ○ Ovate (egg-shaped)
○ Palm and Maple   ○ Lobed

Structure:  ○ Simple (attached to twigs or twig stems)
○ Compound (attached to single lead steam)

Notes: _____
_____

## Flowers, Fruits & Seeds

Flower Type:  ○ Single Blooms   ○ Clustered Blooms   ○ Catkins

Fruits / Seeds:  ○ Berries   ○ Apples   ○ Pears   ○ Nuts   ○ Acorns
○ Cones   ○ Capsules   ○ Catkins   ○(Other) _____

Notes: _____
_____

## Leaf Buds & Twigs

Bud Type:  ○ Terminal (grows at tip of a shoot causing shoot to grow longer)
○ Lateral (grow along sides of a shoot causing sideways growth)

Twig Features:  ○ Smooth   ○ Hairy   ○ Spines   ○ Corky Ribs
○(Other) _____

Notes: _____

## Bark

Texture:  ○ Furrowed   ○ Scaly   ○ Peeling   ○ Smooth   ○ Shiny
○ Fissured   ○ Ridges / Depressions   ○ Papery   ○ Warty
○(Other) _____

Color:  ○ Gray   ○ Brown   ○ Cinnamon   ○ White   ○ Silver
○ Green   ○ Copper   ○(Other) _____

Notes: _____

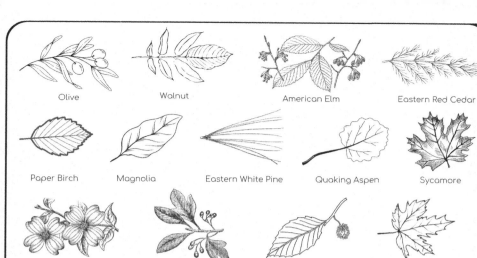

Olive     Walnut     American Elm     Eastern Red Cedar

Paper Birch     Magnolia     Eastern White Pine     Quaking Aspen     Sycamore

Flowering Dogwood     Sassafras     American Beech     Sugar Maple

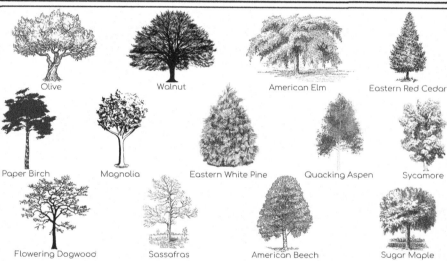

Olive     Walnut     American Elm     Eastern Red Cedar

Paper Birch     Magnolia     Eastern White Pine     Quacking Aspen     Sycamore

Flowering Dogwood     Sassafras     American Beech     Sugar Maple

## Environment

Location / GPS: _____ Date _____

Season: ◯ Spring  ◯ Summer  ◯ Fall  ◯ Winter

Surroundings: ◯ Hedgerows  ◯ Field  ◯ Park  ◯ Woodland  ◯ Water
◯ Other _____

Setting: ◯ Natural  ◯ Artificial   Type: ◯ Evergreen  ◯ Deciduous

Notes: _____
_____

## General

Shape: ◯ Vase  ◯ Columnar  ◯ Round  ◯ (Other) _____

Features: ◯ Conical/Spire  ◯ Spreading  ◯ Upright  ◯ Weeping
◯ (Other) _____

Branching: ◯ Opposite  ◯ Alternate   Estimated Age: _____

Notes: _____
_____

## Needles or Leaves

Type: ◯ Needle  ◯ Simple Broadleaf  ◯ Compound Broadleaf  ◯ Scales

Shape: ◯ Cordate (heart-shaped)  ◯ Lanceolate (long and narrow)
◯ Deltoid (triangular)  ◯ Obicular (round)  ◯ Ovate (egg-shaped)
◯ Palm and Maple  ◯ Lobed

Structure: ◯ Simple (attached to twigs or twig stems)
◯ Compound (attached to single lead steam)

Notes: _____
_____

## Flowers, Fruits & Seeds

Flower Type: ◯ Single Blooms  ◯ Clustered Blooms  ◯ Catkins

Fruits / Seeds: ◯ Berries  ◯ Apples  ◯ Pears  ◯ Nuts  ◯ Acorns
◯ Cones  ◯ Capsules  ◯ Catkins  ◯ (Other) _____

Notes: _____
_____

## Leaf Buds & Twigs

Bud Type: ◯ Terminal (grows at tip of a shoot causing shoot to grow longer)
◯ Lateral (grow along sides of a shoot causing sideways growth)

Twig Features: ◯ Smooth  ◯ Hairy  ◯ Spines  ◯ Corky Ribs
◯ (Other) _____

Notes: _____

## Bark

Texture: ◯ Furrowed  ◯ Scaly  ◯ Peeling  ◯ Smooth  ◯ Shiny
◯ Fissured  ◯ Ridges / Depressions  ◯ Papery  ◯ Warty
◯ (Other) _____

Color: ◯ Gray  ◯ Brown  ◯ Cinnamon  ◯ White  ◯ Silver
◯ Green  ◯ Copper  ◯ (Other) _____

Notes: _____

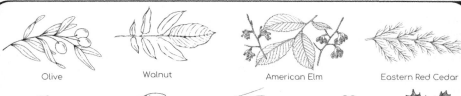

Olive

Walnut

American Elm

Eastern Red Cedar

Paper Birch

Magnolia

Eastern White Pine

Quaking Aspen

Sycamore

Flowering Dogwood

Sassafras

American Beech

Sugar Maple

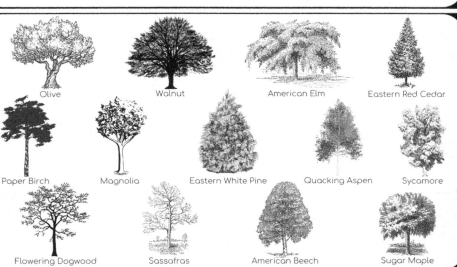

Olive

Walnut

American Elm

Eastern Red Cedar

Paper Birch

Magnolia

Eastern White Pine

Quacking Aspen

Sycamore

Flowering Dogwood

Sassafras

American Beech

Sugar Maple

## Environment

Location / GPS: _____ Date _____

Season: ○ Spring ○ Summer ○ Fall ○ Winter

Surroundings: ○ Hedgerows ○ Field ○ Park ○ Woodland ○ Water
○ Other_____

Setting: ○ Natural ○ Artificial Type: ○ Evergreen ○ Deciduous

Notes: _____
_____

## General

Shape: ○ Vase ○ Columnar ○ Round ○ (Other) _____

Features: ○ Conical/Spire ○ Spreading ○ Upright ○ Weeping
○ (Other) _____

Branching: ○ Opposite ○ Alternate Estimated Age: _____

Notes: _____
_____

## Needles or Leaves

Type: ○ Needle ○ Simple Broadleaf ○ Compound Broadleaf ○ Scales

Shape: ○ Cordate (heart-shaped) ○ Lanceolate (long and narrow)
○ Deltoid (triangular) ○ Obicular (round) ○ Ovate (egg-shaped)
○ Palm and Maple ○ Lobed

Structure: ○ Simple (attached to twigs or twig stems)
○ Compound (attached to single lead steam)

Notes: _____
_____

## Flowers, Fruits & Seeds

Flower Type: ○ Single Blooms ○ Clustered Blooms ○ Catkins

Fruits / Seeds: ○ Berries ○ Apples ○ Pears ○ Nuts ○ Acorns
○ Cones ○ Capsules ○ Catkins ○ (Other) _____

Notes: _____
_____

## Leaf Buds & Twigs

Bud Type: ○ Terminal (grows at tip of a shoot causing shoot to grow longer)
○ Lateral (grow along sides of a shoot causing sideways growth)

Twig Features: ○ Smooth ○ Hairy ○ Spines ○ Corky Ribs
○ (Other) _____

Notes: _____

## Bark

Texture: ○ Furrowed ○ Scaly ○ Peeling ○ Smooth ○ Shiny
○ Fissured ○ Ridges / Depressions ○ Papery ○ Warty
○ (Other) _____

Color: ○ Gray ○ Brown ○ Cinnamon ○ White ○ Silver
○ Green ○ Copper ○ (Other) _____

Notes: _____

Olive

Walnut

American Elm

Eastern Red Cedar

Paper Birch

Magnolia

Eastern White Pine

Quaking Aspen

Sycamore

Flowering Dogwood

Sassafras

American Beech

Sugar Maple

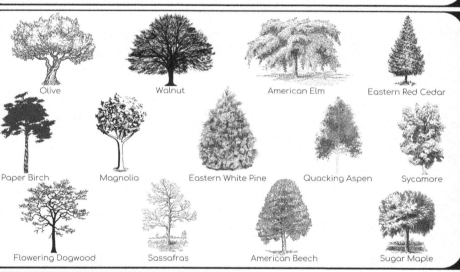

Olive

Walnut

American Elm

Eastern Red Cedar

Paper Birch

Magnolia

Eastern White Pine

Quacking Aspen

Sycamore

Flowering Dogwood

Sassafras

American Beech

Sugar Maple

Location / GPS: _____ Date _____

Season: ○ Spring   ○ Summer   ○ Fall   ○ Winter

Surroundings: ○ Hedgerows  ○ Field  ○ Park  ○ Woodland  ○ Water
○ Other_____

Setting: ○ Natural   ○ Artificial      Type: ○ Evergreen   ○ Deciduous

Notes: _____
_____

Shape: ○ Vase  ○ Columnar  ○ Round  ○ (Other) _____

Features: ○ Conical/Spire  ○ Spreading  ○ Upright  ○ Weeping
○ (Other) _____

Branching: ○ Opposite   ○ Alternate      Estimated Age: _____

Notes: _____
_____

Type: ○ Needle  ○ Simple Broadleaf  ○ Compound Broadleaf  ○ Scales

Shape: ○ Cordate (heart-shaped)   ○ Lanceolate (long and narrow)
○ Deltoid (triangular)  ○ Obicular (round)   ○ Ovate (egg-shaped)
○ Palm and Maple   ○ Lobed

Structure: ○ Simple (attached to twigs or twig stems)
○ Compound (attached to single lead steam)

Notes: _____
_____

Flower Type: ○ Single Blooms   ○ Clustered Blooms   ○ Catkins

Fruits / Seeds: ○ Berries  ○ Apples  ○ Pears  ○ Nuts  ○ Acorns
○ Cones  ○ Capsules  ○ Catkins  ○ (Other) _____

Notes: _____
_____

Bud Type: ○ Terminal (grows at tip of a shoot causing shoot to grow longer)
○ Lateral (grow along sides of a shoot causing sideways growth)

Twig Features: ○ Smooth  ○ Hairy   ○ Spines   ○ Corky Ribs
○ (Other) _____

Notes: _____

Texture: ○ Furrowed  ○ Scaly  ○ Peeling  ○ Smooth  ○ Shiny
○ Fissured  ○ Ridges / Depressions  ○ Papery  ○ Warty
○ (Other) _____

Color: ○ Gray  ○ Brown  ○ Cinnamon  ○ White  ○ Silver
○ Green  ○ Copper  ○ (Other) _____

Notes: _____

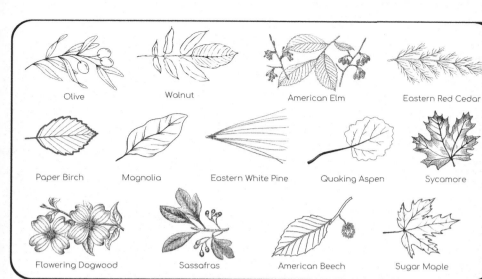

Olive

Walnut

American Elm

Eastern Red Cedar

Paper Birch

Magnolia

Eastern White Pine

Quaking Aspen

Sycamore

Flowering Dogwood

Sassafras

American Beech

Sugar Maple

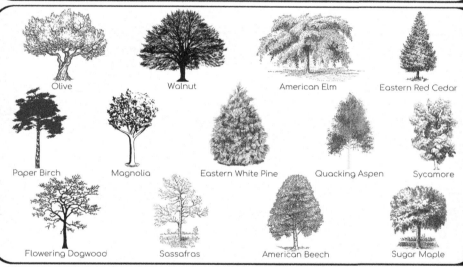

Olive

Walnut

American Elm

Eastern Red Cedar

Paper Birch

Magnolia

Eastern White Pine

Quacking Aspen

Sycamore

Flowering Dogwood

Sassafras

American Beech

Sugar Maple

## Environment

Location / GPS: _____ Date _____

Season: ○ Spring ○ Summer ○ Fall ○ Winter

Surroundings: ○ Hedgerows ○ Field ○ Park ○ Woodland ○ Water
○ Other _____

Setting: ○ Natural ○ Artificial    Type: ○ Evergreen ○ Deciduous

Notes: _____
_____

## General

Shape: ○ Vase ○ Columnar ○ Round ○ (Other) _____

Features: ○ Conical/Spire ○ Spreading ○ Upright ○ Weeping
○ (Other) _____

Branching: ○ Opposite ○ Alternate    Estimated Age: _____

Notes: _____
_____

## Needles or Leaves

Type: ○ Needle ○ Simple Broadleaf ○ Compound Broadleaf ○ Scales

Shape: ○ Cordate (heart-shaped) ○ Lanceolate (long and narrow)
○ Deltoid (triangular) ○ Obicular (round) ○ Ovate (egg-shaped)
○ Palm and Maple ○ Lobed

Structure: ○ Simple (attached to twigs or twig stems)
○ Compound (attached to single lead steam)

Notes: _____
_____

## Flowers, Fruits & Seeds

Flower Type: ○ Single Blooms ○ Clustered Blooms ○ Catkins

Fruits / Seeds: ○ Berries ○ Apples ○ Pears ○ Nuts ○ Acorns
○ Cones ○ Capsules ○ Catkins ○ (Other) _____

Notes: _____
_____

## Leaf Buds & Twigs

Bud Type: ○ Terminal (grows at tip of a shoot causing shoot to grow longer)
○ Lateral (grow along sides of a shoot causing sideways growth)

Twig Features: ○ Smooth ○ Hairy ○ Spines ○ Corky Ribs
○ (Other) _____

Notes: _____

## Bark

Texture: ○ Furrowed ○ Scaly ○ Peeling ○ Smooth ○ Shiny
○ Fissured ○ Ridges / Depressions ○ Papery ○ Warty
○ (Other) _____

Color: ○ Gray ○ Brown ○ Cinnamon ○ White ○ Silver
○ Green ○ Copper ○ (Other) _____

Notes: _____

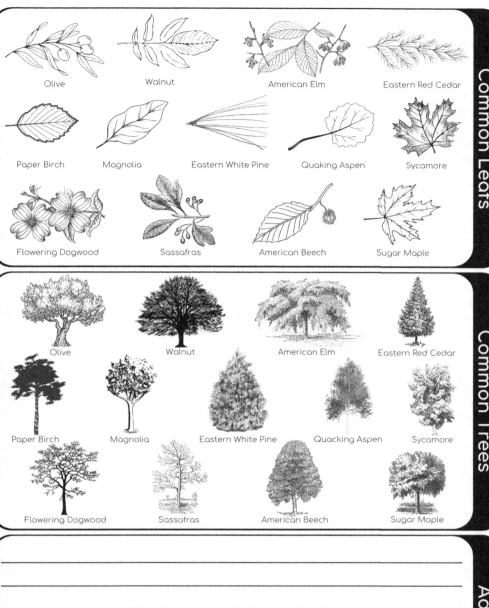

Olive

Walnut

American Elm

Eastern Red Cedar

Paper Birch

Magnolia

Eastern White Pine

Quaking Aspen

Sycamore

Flowering Dogwood

Sassafras

American Beech

Sugar Maple

Olive

Walnut

American Elm

Eastern Red Cedar

Paper Birch

Magnolia

Eastern White Pine

Quacking Aspen

Sycamore

Flowering Dogwood

Sassafras

American Beech

Sugar Maple

## Environment

Location / GPS: _____ Date _____

Season: ○ Spring ○ Summer ○ Fall ○ Winter

Surroundings: ○ Hedgerows ○ Field ○ Park ○ Woodland ○ Water
○ Other_____

Setting: ○ Natural ○ Artificial  Type: ○ Evergreen ○ Deciduous

Notes: _____
_____

## General

Shape: ○ Vase ○ Columnar ○ Round ○ (Other) _____

Features: ○ Conical/Spire ○ Spreading ○ Upright ○ Weeping
○ (Other) _____

Branching: ○ Opposite ○ Alternate  Estimated Age: _____

Notes: _____
_____

## Needles or Leaves

Type: ○ Needle ○ Simple Broadleaf ○ Compound Broadleaf ○ Scales

Shape: ○ Cordate (heart-shaped) ○ Lanceolate (long and narrow)
○ Deltoid (triangular) ○ Obicular (round) ○ Ovate (egg-shaped)
○ Palm and Maple ○ Lobed

Structure: ○ Simple (attached to twigs or twig stems)
○ Compound (attached to single lead steam)

Notes: _____
_____

## Flowers, Fruits & Seeds

Flower Type: ○ Single Blooms ○ Clustered Blooms ○ Catkins

Fruits / Seeds: ○ Berries ○ Apples ○ Pears ○ Nuts ○ Acorns
○ Cones ○ Capsules ○ Catkins ○ (Other) _____

Notes: _____
_____

## Leaf Buds & Twigs

Bud Type: ○ Terminal (grows at tip of a shoot causing shoot to grow longer)
○ Lateral (grow along sides of a shoot causing sideways growth)

Twig Features: ○ Smooth ○ Hairy ○ Spines ○ Corky Ribs
○ (Other) _____

Notes: _____

## Bark

Texture: ○ Furrowed ○ Scaly ○ Peeling ○ Smooth ○ Shiny
○ Fissured ○ Ridges / Depressions ○ Papery ○ Warty
○ (Other) _____

Color: ○ Gray ○ Brown ○ Cinnamon ○ White ○ Silver
○ Green ○ Copper ○ (Other) _____

Notes: _____

Olive     Walnut     American Elm     Eastern Red Cedar

Paper Birch     Magnolia     Eastern White Pine     Quaking Aspen     Sycamore

Flowering Dogwood     Sassafras     American Beech     Sugar Maple

Olive     Walnut     American Elm     Eastern Red Cedar

Paper Birch     Magnolia     Eastern White Pine     Quacking Aspen     Sycamore

Flowering Dogwood     Sassafras     American Beech     Sugar Maple

## Environment

Location / GPS: _____ Date _____

Season: ○ Spring ○ Summer ○ Fall ○ Winter

Surroundings: ○ Hedgerows ○ Field ○ Park ○ Woodland ○ Water
○ Other _____

Setting: ○ Natural ○ Artificial **Type:** ○ Evergreen ○ Deciduous

Notes: _____
_____

## General

Shape: ○ Vase ○ Columnar ○ Round ○ (Other) _____

Features: ○ Conical/Spire ○ Spreading ○ Upright ○ Weeping
○ (Other) _____

Branching: ○ Opposite ○ Alternate **Estimated Age:** _____

Notes: _____
_____

## Needles or Leaves

Type: ○ Needle ○ Simple Broadleaf ○ Compound Broadleaf ○ Scales

Shape: ○ Cordate (heart-shaped) ○ Lanceolate (long and narrow)
○ Deltoid (triangular) ○ Obicular (round) ○ Ovate (egg-shaped)
○ Palm and Maple ○ Lobed

Structure: ○ Simple (attached to twigs or twig stems)
○ Compound (attached to single lead steam)

Notes: _____
_____

## Flowers, Fruits & Seeds

Flower Type: ○ Single Blooms ○ Clustered Blooms ○ Catkins

Fruits / Seeds: ○ Berries ○ Apples ○ Pears ○ Nuts ○ Acorns
○ Cones ○ Capsules ○ Catkins ○ (Other) _____

Notes: _____
_____

## Leaf Buds & Twigs

Bud Type: ○ Terminal (grows at tip of a shoot causing shoot to grow longer)
○ Lateral (grow along sides of a shoot causing sideways growth)

Twig Features: ○ Smooth ○ Hairy ○ Spines ○ Corky Ribs
○ (Other) _____

Notes: _____

## Bark

Texture: ○ Furrowed ○ Scaly ○ Peeling ○ Smooth ○ Shiny
○ Fissured ○ Ridges / Depressions ○ Papery ○ Warty
○ (Other) _____

Color: ○ Gray ○ Brown ○ Cinnamon ○ White ○ Silver
○ Green ○ Copper ○ (Other) _____

Notes: _____

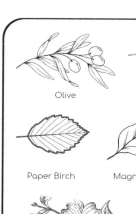

Olive

Walnut

American Elm

Eastern Red Cedar

Paper Birch

Magnolia

Eastern White Pine

Quaking Aspen

Sycamore

Flowering Dogwood

Sassafras

American Beech

Sugar Maple

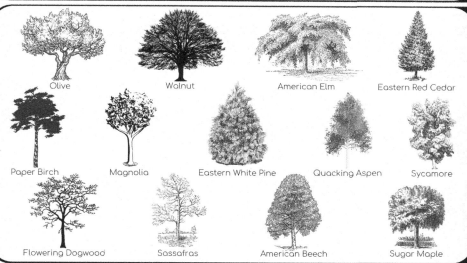

Olive

Walnut

American Elm

Eastern Red Cedar

Paper Birch

Magnolia

Eastern White Pine

Quacking Aspen

Sycamore

Flowering Dogwood

Sassafras

American Beech

Sugar Maple

_____
_____
_____
_____
_____
_____
_____
_____
_____
_____

## Environment

Location / GPS: _____  Date _____

Season:  ○ Spring    ○ Summer    ○ Fall    ○ Winter

Surroundings:  ○ Hedgerows  ○ Field  ○ Park  ○ Woodland  ○ Water
           ○ Other _____

Setting:  ○ Natural   ○ Artificial     Type:  ○ Evergreen   ○ Deciduous

Notes: _____
_____

## General

Shape:  ○ Vase  ○ Columnar  ○ Round  ○ (Other) _____

Features:  ○ Conical/Spire  ○ Spreading  ○ Upright  ○ Weeping
           ○ (Other) _____

Branching:  ○ Opposite  ○ Alternate     Estimated Age: _____

Notes: _____
_____

## Needles or Leaves

Type:  ○ Needle  ○ Simple Broadleaf  ○ Compound Broadleaf  ○ Scales

Shape:  ○ Cordate (heart-shaped)   ○ Lanceolate (long and narrow)
        ○ Deltoid (triangular)  ○ Obicular (round)  ○ Ovate (egg-shaped)
        ○ Palm and Maple  ○ Lobed

Structure:  ○ Simple (attached to twigs or twig stems)
            ○ Compound (attached to single lead steam)

Notes: _____
_____

## Flowers, Fruits & Seeds

Flower Type:  ○ Single Blooms   ○ Clustered Blooms   ○ Catkins

Fruits / Seeds:  ○ Berries  ○ Apples  ○ Pears  ○ Nuts  ○ Acorns
             ○ Cones  ○ Capsules  ○ Catkins  ○ (Other) _____

Notes: _____
_____

## Leaf Buds & Twigs

Bud Type:  ○ Terminal (grows at tip of a shoot causing shoot to grow longer)
           ○ Lateral (grow along sides of a shoot causing sideways growth)

Twig Features:  ○ Smooth  ○ Hairy  ○ Spines  ○ Corky Ribs
            ○ (Other) _____

Notes: _____

## Bark

Texture:  ○ Furrowed  ○ Scaly  ○ Peeling  ○ Smooth  ○ Shiny
          ○ Fissured  ○ Ridges / Depressions  ○ Papery  ○ Warty
          ○ (Other) _____

Color:  ○ Gray  ○ Brown  ○ Cinnamon  ○ White  ○ Silver
        ○ Green  ○ Copper  ○ (Other) _____

Notes: _____

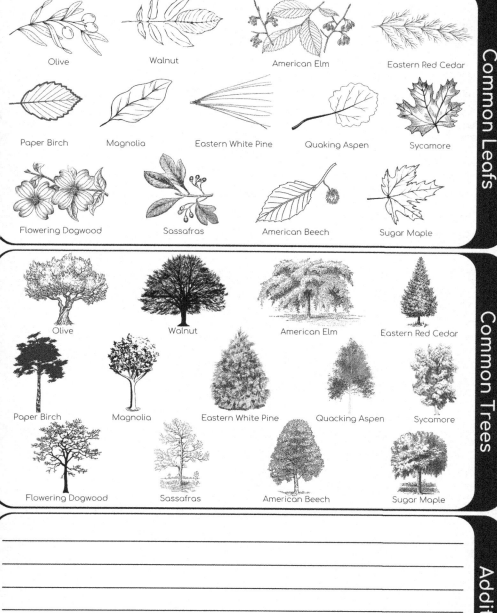

Olive

Walnut

American Elm

Eastern Red Cedar

Paper Birch

Magnolia

Eastern White Pine

Quaking Aspen

Sycamore

Flowering Dogwood

Sassafras

American Beech

Sugar Maple

Olive

Walnut

American Elm

Eastern Red Cedar

Paper Birch

Magnolia

Eastern White Pine

Quacking Aspen

Sycamore

Flowering Dogwood

Sassafras

American Beech

Sugar Maple

## Environment

Location / GPS: _____ Date _____

Season: ◯ Spring ◯ Summer ◯ Fall ◯ Winter

Surroundings: ◯ Hedgerows ◯ Field ◯ Park ◯ Woodland ◯ Water
◯ Other _____

Setting: ◯ Natural ◯ Artificial   Type: ◯ Evergreen ◯ Deciduous

Notes: _____
_____

## General

Shape: ◯ Vase ◯ Columnar ◯ Round ◯ (Other) _____

Features: ◯ Conical/Spire ◯ Spreading ◯ Upright ◯ Weeping
◯ (Other) _____

Branching: ◯ Opposite ◯ Alternate   Estimated Age: _____

Notes: _____
_____

## Needles or Leaves

Type: ◯ Needle ◯ Simple Broadleaf ◯ Compound Broadleaf ◯ Scales

Shape: ◯ Cordate (heart-shaped) ◯ Lanceolate (long and narrow)
◯ Deltoid (triangular) ◯ Obicular (round) ◯ Ovate (egg-shaped)
◯ Palm and Maple ◯ Lobed

Structure: ◯ Simple (attached to twigs or twig stems)
◯ Compound (attached to single lead steam)

Notes: _____
_____

## Flowers, Fruits & Seeds

Flower Type: ◯ Single Blooms ◯ Clustered Blooms ◯ Catkins

Fruits / Seeds: ◯ Berries ◯ Apples ◯ Pears ◯ Nuts ◯ Acorns
◯ Cones ◯ Capsules ◯ Catkins ◯ (Other) _____

Notes: _____
_____

## Leaf Buds & Twigs

Bud Type: ◯ Terminal (grows at tip of a shoot causing shoot to grow longer)
◯ Lateral (grow along sides of a shoot causing sideways growth)

Twig Features: ◯ Smooth ◯ Hairy ◯ Spines ◯ Corky Ribs
◯ (Other) _____

Notes: _____

## Bark

Texture: ◯ Furrowed ◯ Scaly ◯ Peeling ◯ Smooth ◯ Shiny
◯ Fissured ◯ Ridges / Depressions ◯ Papery ◯ Warty
◯ (Other) _____

Color: ◯ Gray ◯ Brown ◯ Cinnamon ◯ White ◯ Silver
◯ Green ◯ Copper ◯ (Other) _____

Notes: _____

Olive

Walnut

American Elm

Eastern Red Cedar

Paper Birch

Magnolia

Eastern White Pine

Quaking Aspen

Sycamore

Flowering Dogwood

Sassafras

American Beech

Sugar Maple

Olive

Walnut

American Elm

Eastern Red Cedar

Paper Birch

Magnolia

Eastern White Pine

Quacking Aspen

Sycamore

Flowering Dogwood

Sassafras

American Beech

Sugar Maple

## Environment

Location / GPS: _____ Date _____

Season:  ○ Spring   ○ Summer   ○ Fall   ○ Winter

Surroundings:  ○ Hedgerows  ○ Field  ○ Park  ○ Woodland  ○ Water
○ Other _____

Setting:  ○ Natural  ○ Artificial   Type:  ○ Evergreen   ○ Deciduous

Notes: _____
_____

## General

Shape:  ○ Vase  ○ Columnar  ○ Round  ○ (Other) _____

Features:  ○ Conical/Spire  ○ Spreading  ○ Upright  ○ Weeping
○ (Other) _____

Branching:  ○ Opposite   ○ Alternate     Estimated Age: _____

Notes: _____
_____

## Needles or Leaves

Type:  ○ Needle  ○ Simple Broadleaf  ○ Compound Broadleaf  ○ Scales

Shape:  ○ Cordate (heart-shaped)   ○ Lanceolate (long and narrow)
○ Deltoid (triangular)  ○ Obicular (round)  ○ Ovate (egg-shaped)
○ Palm and Maple  ○ Lobed

Structure:  ○ Simple (attached to twigs or twig stems)
○ Compound (attached to single lead steam)

Notes: _____
_____

## Flowers, Fruits & Seeds

Flower Type:  ○ Single Blooms  ○ Clustered Blooms  ○ Catkins

Fruits / Seeds:  ○ Berries  ○ Apples  ○ Pears  ○ Nuts  ○ Acorns
○ Cones  ○ Capsules  ○ Catkins  ○ (Other) _____

Notes: _____
_____

## Leaf Buds & Twigs

Bud Type:  ○ Terminal (grows at tip of a shoot causing shoot to grow longer)
○ Lateral (grow along sides of a shoot causing sideways growth)

Twig Features:  ○ Smooth  ○ Hairy  ○ Spines  ○ Corky Ribs
○ (Other) _____

Notes: _____

## Bark

Texture:  ○ Furrowed  ○ Scaly  ○ Peeling  ○ Smooth  ○ Shiny
○ Fissured  ○ Ridges / Depressions  ○ Papery  ○ Warty
○ (Other) _____

Color:  ○ Gray  ○ Brown  ○ Cinnamon  ○ White  ○ Silver
○ Green  ○ Copper  ○ (Other) _____

Notes: _____

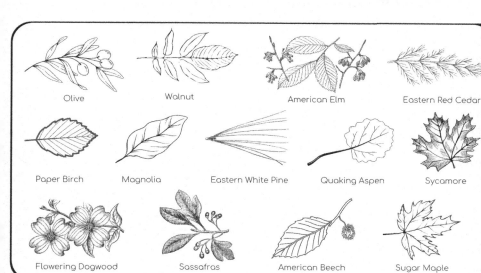

Olive | Walnut | American Elm | Eastern Red Cedar

Paper Birch | Magnolia | Eastern White Pine | Quaking Aspen | Sycamore

Flowering Dogwood | Sassafras | American Beech | Sugar Maple

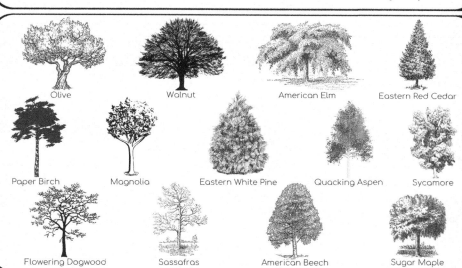

Olive | Walnut | American Elm | Eastern Red Cedar

Paper Birch | Magnolia | Eastern White Pine | Quacking Aspen | Sycamore

Flowering Dogwood | Sassafras | American Beech | Sugar Maple

## Environment

Location / GPS: _____ Date _____

Season: ◯ Spring ◯ Summer ◯ Fall ◯ Winter

Surroundings: ◯ Hedgerows ◯ Field ◯ Park ◯ Woodland ◯ Water
◯ Other _____

Setting: ◯ Natural ◯ Artificial    Type: ◯ Evergreen ◯ Deciduous

Notes: _____
_____

## General

Shape: ◯ Vase ◯ Columnar ◯ Round ◯ (Other) _____

Features: ◯ Conical/Spire ◯ Spreading ◯ Upright ◯ Weeping
◯ (Other) _____

Branching: ◯ Opposite ◯ Alternate    Estimated Age: _____

Notes: _____
_____

## Needles or Leaves

Type: ◯ Needle ◯ Simple Broadleaf ◯ Compound Broadleaf ◯ Scales

Shape: ◯ Cordate (heart-shaped) ◯ Lanceolate (long and narrow)
◯ Deltoid (triangular) ◯ Obicular (round) ◯ Ovate (egg-shaped)
◯ Palm and Maple ◯ Lobed

Structure: ◯ Simple (attached to twigs or twig stems)
◯ Compound (attached to single lead steam)

Notes: _____
_____

## Flowers, Fruits & Seeds

Flower Type: ◯ Single Blooms ◯ Clustered Blooms ◯ Catkins

Fruits / Seeds: ◯ Berries ◯ Apples ◯ Pears ◯ Nuts ◯ Acorns
◯ Cones ◯ Capsules ◯ Catkins ◯ (Other) _____

Notes: _____
_____

## Leaf Buds & Twigs

Bud Type: ◯ Terminal (grows at tip of a shoot causing shoot to grow longer)
◯ Lateral (grow along sides of a shoot causing sideways growth)

Twig Features: ◯ Smooth ◯ Hairy ◯ Spines ◯ Corky Ribs
◯ (Other) _____

Notes: _____

## Bark

Texture: ◯ Furrowed ◯ Scaly ◯ Peeling ◯ Smooth ◯ Shiny
◯ Fissured ◯ Ridges / Depressions ◯ Papery ◯ Warty
◯ (Other) _____

Color: ◯ Gray ◯ Brown ◯ Cinnamon ◯ White ◯ Silver
◯ Green ◯ Copper ◯ (Other) _____

Notes: _____

Olive

Walnut

American Elm

Eastern Red Cedar

Paper Birch

Magnolia

Eastern White Pine

Quaking Aspen

Sycamore

Flowering Dogwood

Sassafras

American Beech

Sugar Maple

Olive

Walnut

American Elm

Eastern Red Cedar

Paper Birch

Magnolia

Eastern White Pine

Quacking Aspen

Sycamore

Flowering Dogwood

Sassafras

American Beech

Sugar Maple

## Environment

Location / GPS: _____ Date _____

Season: ◯ Spring  ◯ Summer  ◯ Fall  ◯ Winter

Surroundings: ◯ Hedgerows  ◯ Field  ◯ Park  ◯ Woodland  ◯ Water
◯ Other _____

Setting: ◯ Natural  ◯ Artificial   Type: ◯ Evergreen  ◯ Deciduous

Notes: _____
_____

## General

Shape: ◯ Vase  ◯ Columnar  ◯ Round  ◯ (Other) _____

Features: ◯ Conical/Spire  ◯ Spreading  ◯ Upright  ◯ Weeping
◯ (Other) _____

Branching: ◯ Opposite  ◯ Alternate   Estimated Age: _____

Notes: _____
_____

## Needles or Leaves

Type: ◯ Needle  ◯ Simple Broadleaf  ◯ Compound Broadleaf  ◯ Scales

Shape: ◯ Cordate (heart-shaped)  ◯ Lanceolate (long and narrow)
◯ Deltoid (triangular)  ◯ Obicular (round)  ◯ Ovate (egg-shaped)
◯ Palm and Maple  ◯ Lobed

Structure: ◯ Simple (attached to twigs or twig stems)
◯ Compound (attached to single lead steam)

Notes: _____
_____

## Flowers, Fruits & Seeds

Flower Type: ◯ Single Blooms  ◯ Clustered Blooms  ◯ Catkins

Fruits / Seeds: ◯ Berries  ◯ Apples  ◯ Pears  ◯ Nuts  ◯ Acorns
◯ Cones  ◯ Capsules  ◯ Catkins  ◯ (Other) _____

Notes: _____
_____

## Leaf Buds & Twigs

Bud Type: ◯ Terminal (grows at tip of a shoot causing shoot to grow longer)
◯ Lateral (grow along sides of a shoot causing sideways growth)

Twig Features: ◯ Smooth  ◯ Hairy  ◯ Spines  ◯ Corky Ribs
◯ (Other) _____

Notes: _____

## Bark

Texture: ◯ Furrowed  ◯ Scaly  ◯ Peeling  ◯ Smooth  ◯ Shiny
◯ Fissured  ◯ Ridges / Depressions  ◯ Papery  ◯ Warty
◯ (Other) _____

Color: ◯ Gray  ◯ Brown  ◯ Cinnamon  ◯ White  ◯ Silver
◯ Green  ◯ Copper  ◯ (Other) _____

Notes: _____

Olive

Walnut

American Elm

Eastern Red Cedar

Paper Birch

Magnolia

Eastern White Pine

Quaking Aspen

Sycamore

Flowering Dogwood

Sassafras

American Beech

Sugar Maple

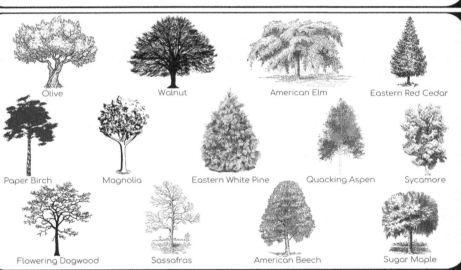

Olive

Walnut

American Elm

Eastern Red Cedar

Paper Birch

Magnolia

Eastern White Pine

Quacking Aspen

Sycamore

Flowering Dogwood

Sassafras

American Beech

Sugar Maple

## Environment

Location / GPS: _____ Date _____

Season: ○ Spring ○ Summer ○ Fall ○ Winter

Surroundings: ○ Hedgerows ○ Field ○ Park ○ Woodland ○ Water
○ Other _____

Setting: ○ Natural ○ Artificial **Type:** ○ Evergreen ○ Deciduous

Notes: _____
_____

## General

Shape: ○ Vase ○ Columnar ○ Round ○ (Other) _____

Features: ○ Conical/Spire ○ Spreading ○ Upright ○ Weeping
○ (Other) _____

Branching: ○ Opposite ○ Alternate **Estimated Age:** _____

Notes: _____
_____

## Needles or Leaves

Type: ○ Needle ○ Simple Broadleaf ○ Compound Broadleaf ○ Scales

Shape: ○ Cordate (heart-shaped) ○ Lanceolate (long and narrow)
○ Deltoid (triangular) ○ Obicular (round) ○ Ovate (egg-shaped)
○ Palm and Maple ○ Lobed

Structure: ○ Simple (attached to twigs or twig stems)
○ Compound (attached to single lead steam)

Notes: _____
_____

## Flowers, Fruits & Seeds

Flower Type: ○ Single Blooms ○ Clustered Blooms ○ Catkins

Fruits / Seeds: ○ Berries ○ Apples ○ Pears ○ Nuts ○ Acorns
○ Cones ○ Capsules ○ Catkins ○ (Other) _____

Notes: _____
_____

## Leaf Buds & Twigs

Bud Type: ○ Terminal (grows at tip of a shoot causing shoot to grow longer)
○ Lateral (grow along sides of a shoot causing sideways growth)

Twig Features: ○ Smooth ○ Hairy ○ Spines ○ Corky Ribs
○ (Other) _____

Notes: _____

## Bark

Texture: ○ Furrowed ○ Scaly ○ Peeling ○ Smooth ○ Shiny
○ Fissured ○ Ridges / Depressions ○ Papery ○ Warty
○ (Other) _____

Color: ○ Gray ○ Brown ○ Cinnamon ○ White ○ Silver
○ Green ○ Copper ○ (Other) _____

Notes: _____

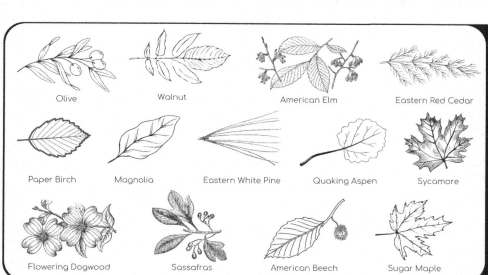

Olive • Walnut • American Elm • Eastern Red Cedar

Paper Birch • Magnolia • Eastern White Pine • Quaking Aspen • Sycamore

Flowering Dogwood • Sassafras • American Beech • Sugar Maple

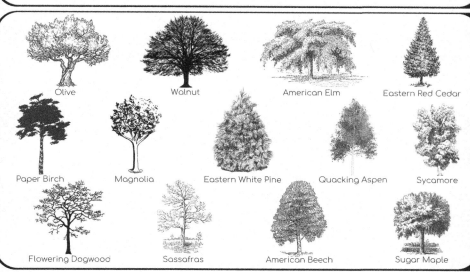

Olive • Walnut • American Elm • Eastern Red Cedar

Paper Birch • Magnolia • Eastern White Pine • Quacking Aspen • Sycamore

Flowering Dogwood • Sassafras • American Beech • Sugar Maple

## Environment

Location / GPS: _____ Date _____

Season: ○ Spring ○ Summer ○ Fall ○ Winter

Surroundings: ○ Hedgerows ○ Field ○ Park ○ Woodland ○ Water
○ Other _____

Setting: ○ Natural ○ Artificial     Type: ○ Evergreen ○ Deciduous

Notes: _____
_____

## General

Shape: ○ Vase ○ Columnar ○ Round ○ (Other) _____

Features: ○ Conical/Spire ○ Spreading ○ Upright ○ Weeping
○ (Other) _____

Branching: ○ Opposite ○ Alternate     Estimated Age: _____

Notes: _____
_____

## Needles or Leaves

Type: ○ Needle ○ Simple Broadleaf ○ Compound Broadleaf ○ Scales

Shape: ○ Cordate (heart-shaped) ○ Lanceolate (long and narrow)
○ Deltoid (triangular) ○ Obicular (round) ○ Ovate (egg-shaped)
○ Palm and Maple ○ Lobed

Structure: ○ Simple (attached to twigs or twig stems)
○ Compound (attached to single lead steam)

Notes: _____
_____

## Flowers, Fruits & Seeds

Flower Type: ○ Single Blooms ○ Clustered Blooms ○ Catkins

Fruits / Seeds: ○ Berries ○ Apples ○ Pears ○ Nuts ○ Acorns
○ Cones ○ Capsules ○ Catkins ○ (Other) _____

Notes: _____
_____

## Leaf Buds & Twigs

Bud Type: ○ Terminal (grows at tip of a shoot causing shoot to grow longer)
○ Lateral (grow along sides of a shoot causing sideways growth)

Twig Features: ○ Smooth ○ Hairy ○ Spines ○ Corky Ribs
○ (Other) _____

Notes: _____

## Bark

Texture: ○ Furrowed ○ Scaly ○ Peeling ○ Smooth ○ Shiny
○ Fissured ○ Ridges / Depressions ○ Papery ○ Warty
○ (Other) _____

Color: ○ Gray ○ Brown ○ Cinnamon ○ White ○ Silver
○ Green ○ Copper ○ (Other) _____

Notes: _____

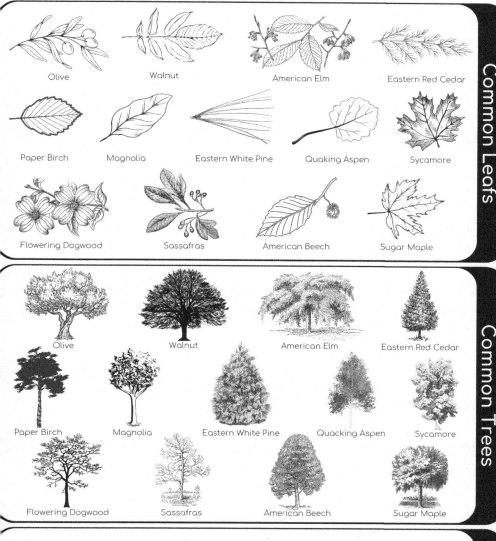

Olive

Walnut

American Elm

Eastern Red Cedar

Paper Birch

Magnolia

Eastern White Pine

Quaking Aspen

Sycamore

Flowering Dogwood

Sassafras

American Beech

Sugar Maple

Olive

Walnut

American Elm

Eastern Red Cedar

Paper Birch

Magnolia

Eastern White Pine

Quacking Aspen

Sycamore

Flowering Dogwood

Sassafras

American Beech

Sugar Maple

## Environment

Location / GPS: _____ Date _____

Season: ○ Spring ○ Summer ○ Fall ○ Winter

Surroundings: ○ Hedgerows ○ Field ○ Park ○ Woodland ○ Water
○ Other _____

Setting: ○ Natural ○ Artificial  Type: ○ Evergreen ○ Deciduous

Notes: _____
_____

## General

Shape: ○ Vase ○ Columnar ○ Round ○ (Other) _____

Features: ○ Conical/Spire ○ Spreading ○ Upright ○ Weeping
○ (Other) _____

Branching: ○ Opposite ○ Alternate  Estimated Age: _____

Notes: _____
_____
_____

## Needles or Leaves

Type: ○ Needle ○ Simple Broadleaf ○ Compound Broadleaf ○ Scales

Shape: ○ Cordate (heart-shaped) ○ Lanceolate (long and narrow)
○ Deltoid (triangular) ○ Obicular (round) ○ Ovate (egg-shaped)
○ Palm and Maple ○ Lobed

Structure: ○ Simple (attached to twigs or twig stems)
○ Compound (attached to single lead steam)

Notes: _____
_____

## Flowers, Fruits & Seeds

Flower Type: ○ Single Blooms ○ Clustered Blooms ○ Catkins

Fruits / Seeds: ○ Berries ○ Apples ○ Pears ○ Nuts ○ Acorns
○ Cones ○ Capsules ○ Catkins ○ (Other) _____

Notes: _____
_____

## Leaf Buds & Twigs

Bud Type: ○ Terminal (grows at tip of a shoot causing shoot to grow longer)
○ Lateral (grow along sides of a shoot causing sideways growth)

Twig Features: ○ Smooth ○ Hairy ○ Spines ○ Corky Ribs
○ (Other) _____

Notes: _____

## Bark

Texture: ○ Furrowed ○ Scaly ○ Peeling ○ Smooth ○ Shiny
○ Fissured ○ Ridges / Depressions ○ Papery ○ Warty
○ (Other) _____

Color: ○ Gray ○ Brown ○ Cinnamon ○ White ○ Silver
○ Green ○ Copper ○ (Other) _____

Notes: _____

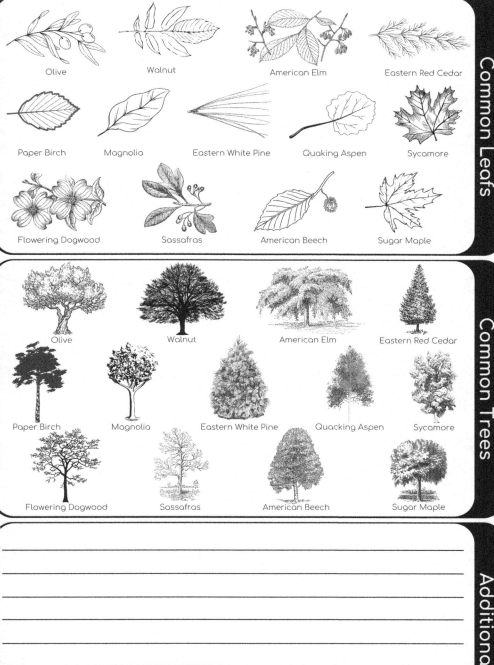

Olive

Walnut

American Elm

Eastern Red Cedar

Paper Birch

Magnolia

Eastern White Pine

Quaking Aspen

Sycamore

Flowering Dogwood

Sassafras

American Beech

Sugar Maple

Olive

Walnut

American Elm

Eastern Red Cedar

Paper Birch

Magnolia

Eastern White Pine

Quacking Aspen

Sycamore

Flowering Dogwood

Sassafras

American Beech

Sugar Maple

## Environment

Location / GPS: _____ Date _____

Season: ○ Spring ○ Summer ○ Fall ○ Winter

Surroundings: ○ Hedgerows ○ Field ○ Park ○ Woodland ○ Water
○ Other _____

Setting: ○ Natural ○ Artificial   Type: ○ Evergreen ○ Deciduous

Notes: _____
_____
_____

## General

Shape: ○ Vase ○ Columnar ○ Round ○ (Other) _____

Features: ○ Conical/Spire ○ Spreading ○ Upright ○ Weeping
○ (Other) _____

Branching: ○ Opposite ○ Alternate   Estimated Age: _____

Notes: _____
_____
_____

## Needles or Leaves

Type: ○ Needle ○ Simple Broadleaf ○ Compound Broadleaf ○ Scales

Shape: ○ Cordate (heart-shaped) ○ Lanceolate (long and narrow)
○ Deltoid (triangular) ○ Obicular (round) ○ Ovate (egg-shaped)
○ Palm and Maple ○ Lobed

Structure: ○ Simple (attached to twigs or twig stems)
○ Compound (attached to single lead steam)

Notes: _____
_____
_____

## Flowers, Fruits & Seeds

Flower Type: ○ Single Blooms ○ Clustered Blooms ○ Catkins

Fruits / Seeds: ○ Berries ○ Apples ○ Pears ○ Nuts ○ Acorns
○ Cones ○ Capsules ○ Catkins ○ (Other) _____

Notes: _____
_____
_____

## Leaf Buds & Twigs

Bud Type: ○ Terminal (grows at tip of a shoot causing shoot to grow longer)
○ Lateral (grow along sides of a shoot causing sideways growth)

Twig Features: ○ Smooth ○ Hairy ○ Spines ○ Corky Ribs
○ (Other) _____

Notes: _____
_____

## Bark

Texture: ○ Furrowed ○ Scaly ○ Peeling ○ Smooth ○ Shiny
○ Fissured ○ Ridges / Depressions ○ Papery ○ Warty
○ (Other) _____

Color: ○ Gray ○ Brown ○ Cinnamon ○ White ○ Silver
○ Green ○ Copper ○ (Other) _____

Notes: _____

Olive

Walnut

American Elm

Eastern Red Cedar

Paper Birch

Magnolia

Eastern White Pine

Quaking Aspen

Sycamore

Flowering Dogwood

Sassafras

American Beech

Sugar Maple

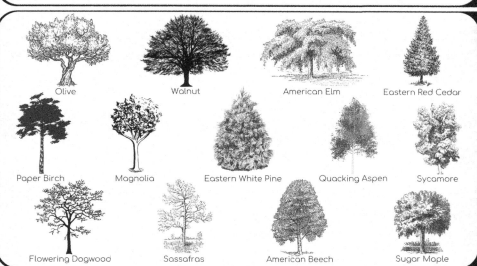

Olive

Walnut

American Elm

Eastern Red Cedar

Paper Birch

Magnolia

Eastern White Pine

Quacking Aspen

Sycamore

Flowering Dogwood

Sassafras

American Beech

Sugar Maple

## Environment

Location / GPS: _____ Date _____

Season:  ○ Spring  ○ Summer  ○ Fall  ○ Winter

Surroundings:  ○ Hedgerows  ○ Field  ○ Park  ○ Woodland  ○ Water
○ Other _____

Setting:  ○ Natural  ○ Artificial  Type:  ○ Evergreen  ○ Deciduous

Notes: _____
_____

## General

Shape:  ○ Vase  ○ Columnar  ○ Round  ○ (Other) _____

Features:  ○ Conical/Spire  ○ Spreading  ○ Upright  ○ Weeping
○ (Other) _____

Branching:  ○ Opposite  ○ Alternate  Estimated Age: _____

Notes: _____
_____

## Needles or Leaves

Type:  ○ Needle  ○ Simple Broadleaf  ○ Compound Broadleaf  ○ Scales

Shape:  ○ Cordate (heart-shaped)  ○ Lanceolate (long and narrow)
○ Deltoid (triangular)  ○ Obicular (round)  ○ Ovate (egg-shaped)
○ Palm and Maple  ○ Lobed

Structure:  ○ Simple (attached to twigs or twig stems)
○ Compound (attached to single lead steam)

Notes: _____
_____

## Flowers, Fruits & Seeds

Flower Type:  ○ Single Blooms  ○ Clustered Blooms  ○ Catkins

Fruits / Seeds:  ○ Berries  ○ Apples  ○ Pears  ○ Nuts  ○ Acorns
○ Cones  ○ Capsules  ○ Catkins  ○ (Other) _____

Notes: _____
_____

## Leaf Buds & Twigs

Bud Type:  ○ Terminal (grows at tip of a shoot causing shoot to grow longer)
○ Lateral (grow along sides of a shoot causing sideways growth)

Twig Features:  ○ Smooth  ○ Hairy  ○ Spines  ○ Corky Ribs
○ (Other) _____

Notes: _____

## Bark

Texture:  ○ Furrowed  ○ Scaly  ○ Peeling  ○ Smooth  ○ Shiny
○ Fissured  ○ Ridges / Depressions  ○ Papery  ○ Warty
○ (Other) _____

Color:  ○ Gray  ○ Brown  ○ Cinnamon  ○ White  ○ Silver
○ Green  ○ Copper  ○ (Other) _____

Notes: _____

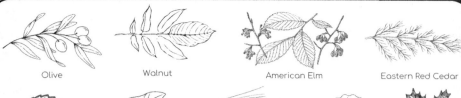

Olive

Walnut

American Elm

Eastern Red Cedar

Paper Birch

Magnolia

Eastern White Pine

Quaking Aspen

Sycamore

Flowering Dogwood

Sassafras

American Beech

Sugar Maple

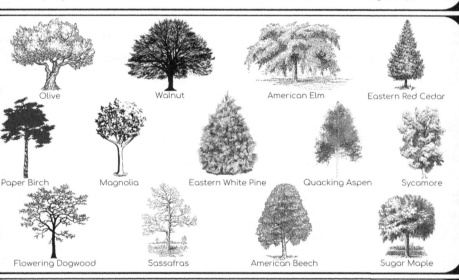

Olive

Walnut

American Elm

Eastern Red Cedar

Paper Birch

Magnolia

Eastern White Pine

Quacking Aspen

Sycamore

Flowering Dogwood

Sassafras

American Beech

Sugar Maple

## Environment

**Location / GPS:** _____ **Date** _____

**Season:** ◯ Spring  ◯ Summer  ◯ Fall  ◯ Winter

**Surroundings:** ◯ Hedgerows  ◯ Field  ◯ Park  ◯ Woodland  ◯ Water
◯ Other _____

**Setting:** ◯ Natural  ◯ Artificial   **Type:** ◯ Evergreen  ◯ Deciduous

**Notes:** _____
_____

## General

**Shape:** ◯ Vase  ◯ Columnar  ◯ Round  ◯ (Other) _____

**Features:** ◯ Conical/Spire  ◯ Spreading  ◯ Upright  ◯ Weeping
◯ (Other) _____

**Branching:** ◯ Opposite  ◯ Alternate   **Estimated Age:** _____

**Notes:** _____
_____

## Needles or Leaves

**Type:** ◯ Needle  ◯ Simple Broadleaf  ◯ Compound Broadleaf  ◯ Scales

**Shape:** ◯ Cordate (heart-shaped)  ◯ Lanceolate (long and narrow)
◯ Deltoid (triangular)  ◯ Obicular (round)  ◯ Ovate (egg-shaped)
◯ Palm and Maple  ◯ Lobed

**Structure:** ◯ Simple (attached to twigs or twig stems)
◯ Compound (attached to single lead steam)

**Notes:** _____
_____

## Flowers, Fruits & Seeds

**Flower Type:** ◯ Single Blooms  ◯ Clustered Blooms  ◯ Catkins

**Fruits / Seeds:** ◯ Berries  ◯ Apples  ◯ Pears  ◯ Nuts  ◯ Acorns
◯ Cones  ◯ Capsules  ◯ Catkins  ◯ (Other) _____

**Notes:** _____
_____

## Leaf Buds & Twigs

**Bud Type:** ◯ Terminal (grows at tip of a shoot causing shoot to grow longer)
◯ Lateral (grow along sides of a shoot causing sideways growth)

**Twig Features:** ◯ Smooth  ◯ Hairy  ◯ Spines  ◯ Corky Ribs
◯ (Other) _____

**Notes:** _____

## Bark

**Texture:** ◯ Furrowed  ◯ Scaly  ◯ Peeling  ◯ Smooth  ◯ Shiny
◯ Fissured  ◯ Ridges / Depressions  ◯ Papery  ◯ Warty
◯ (Other) _____

**Color:** ◯ Gray  ◯ Brown  ◯ Cinnamon  ◯ White  ◯ Silver
◯ Green  ◯ Copper  ◯ (Other) _____

**Notes:** _____

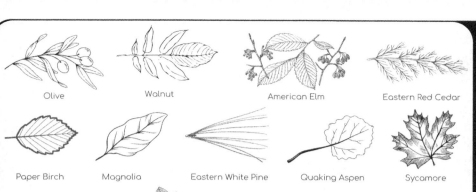

Olive  Walnut  American Elm  Eastern Red Cedar

Paper Birch  Magnolia  Eastern White Pine  Quaking Aspen  Sycamore

Flowering Dogwood  Sassafras  American Beech  Sugar Maple

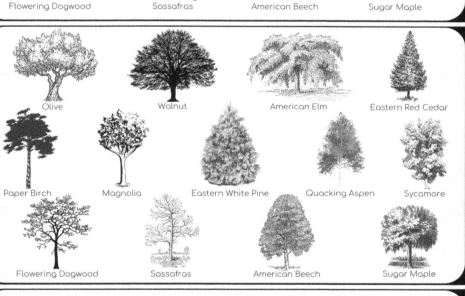

Olive  Walnut  American Elm  Eastern Red Cedar

Paper Birch  Magnolia  Eastern White Pine  Quacking Aspen  Sycamore

Flowering Dogwood  Sassafras  American Beech  Sugar Maple

## Environment

Location / GPS: _____ Date _____

Season: ○ Spring ○ Summer ○ Fall ○ Winter

Surroundings: ○ Hedgerows ○ Field ○ Park ○ Woodland ○ Water
○ Other _____

Setting: ○ Natural ○ Artificial    Type: ○ Evergreen ○ Deciduous

Notes: _____
_____

## General

Shape: ○ Vase ○ Columnar ○ Round ○ (Other) _____

Features: ○ Conical/Spire ○ Spreading ○ Upright ○ Weeping
○ (Other) _____

Branching: ○ Opposite ○ Alternate    Estimated Age: _____

Notes: _____
_____

## Needles or Leaves

Type: ○ Needle ○ Simple Broadleaf ○ Compound Broadleaf ○ Scales

Shape: ○ Cordate (heart-shaped) ○ Lanceolate (long and narrow)
○ Deltoid (triangular) ○ Obicular (round) ○ Ovate (egg-shaped)
○ Palm and Maple ○ Lobed

Structure: ○ Simple (attached to twigs or twig stems)
○ Compound (attached to single lead steam)

Notes: _____
_____

## Flowers, Fruits & Seeds

Flower Type: ○ Single Blooms ○ Clustered Blooms ○ Catkins

Fruits / Seeds: ○ Berries ○ Apples ○ Pears ○ Nuts ○ Acorns
○ Cones ○ Capsules ○ Catkins ○ (Other) _____

Notes: _____
_____

## Leaf Buds & Twigs

Bud Type: ○ Terminal (grows at tip of a shoot causing shoot to grow longer)
○ Lateral (grow along sides of a shoot causing sideways growth)

Twig Features: ○ Smooth ○ Hairy ○ Spines ○ Corky Ribs
○ (Other) _____

Notes: _____

## Bark

Texture: ○ Furrowed ○ Scaly ○ Peeling ○ Smooth ○ Shiny
○ Fissured ○ Ridges / Depressions ○ Papery ○ Warty
○ (Other) _____

Color: ○ Gray ○ Brown ○ Cinnamon ○ White ○ Silver
○ Green ○ Copper ○ (Other) _____

Notes: _____

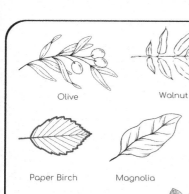

Olive

Walnut

American Elm

Eastern Red Cedar

Paper Birch

Magnolia

Eastern White Pine

Quaking Aspen

Sycamore

Flowering Dogwood

Sassafras

American Beech

Sugar Maple

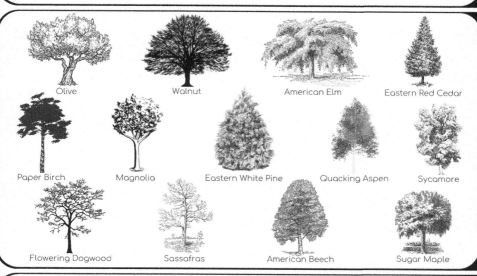

Olive

Walnut

American Elm

Eastern Red Cedar

Paper Birch

Magnolia

Eastern White Pine

Quacking Aspen

Sycamore

Flowering Dogwood

Sassafras

American Beech

Sugar Maple

## Environment

Location / GPS: _____ Date _____

Season: ○ Spring ○ Summer ○ Fall ○ Winter

Surroundings: ○ Hedgerows ○ Field ○ Park ○ Woodland ○ Water
○ Other _____

Setting: ○ Natural ○ Artificial    Type: ○ Evergreen ○ Deciduous

Notes: _____
_____

## General

Shape: ○ Vase ○ Columnar ○ Round ○ (Other) _____

Features: ○ Conical/Spire ○ Spreading ○ Upright ○ Weeping
○ (Other) _____

Branching: ○ Opposite ○ Alternate    Estimated Age: _____

Notes: _____
_____

## Needles or Leaves

Type: ○ Needle ○ Simple Broadleaf ○ Compound Broadleaf ○ Scales

Shape: ○ Cordate (heart-shaped) ○ Lanceolate (long and narrow)
○ Deltoid (triangular) ○ Obicular (round) ○ Ovate (egg-shaped)
○ Palm and Maple ○ Lobed

Structure: ○ Simple (attached to twigs or twig stems)
○ Compound (attached to single lead steam)

Notes: _____
_____

## Flowers, Fruits & Seeds

Flower Type: ○ Single Blooms ○ Clustered Blooms ○ Catkins

Fruits / Seeds: ○ Berries ○ Apples ○ Pears ○ Nuts ○ Acorns
○ Cones ○ Capsules ○ Catkins ○ (Other) _____

Notes: _____
_____

## Leaf Buds & Twigs

Bud Type: ○ Terminal (grows at tip of a shoot causing shoot to grow longer)
○ Lateral (grow along sides of a shoot causing sideways growth)

Twig Features: ○ Smooth ○ Hairy ○ Spines ○ Corky Ribs
○ (Other) _____

Notes: _____

## Bark

Texture: ○ Furrowed ○ Scaly ○ Peeling ○ Smooth ○ Shiny
○ Fissured ○ Ridges / Depressions ○ Papery ○ Warty
○ (Other) _____

Color: ○ Gray ○ Brown ○ Cinnamon ○ White ○ Silver
○ Green ○ Copper ○ (Other) _____

Notes: _____

## Common Leafs

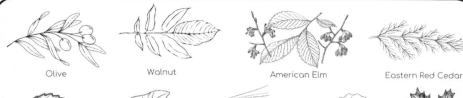

 Olive

 Walnut

 American Elm

 Eastern Red Cedar

 Paper Birch

 Magnolia

 Eastern White Pine

Quaking Aspen

 Sycamore

 Flowering Dogwood

 Sassafras

 American Beech

 Sugar Maple

## Common Trees

 Olive

Walnut

 American Elm

 Eastern Red Cedar

Paper Birch

Magnolia

Eastern White Pine

Quacking Aspen

Sycamore

Flowering Dogwood

Sassafras

American Beech

Sugar Maple

## Additional Notes

## Environment

Location / GPS: _____ Date _____

Season: ○ Spring ○ Summer ○ Fall ○ Winter

Surroundings: ○ Hedgerows ○ Field ○ Park ○ Woodland ○ Water
○ Other_____

Setting: ○ Natural ○ Artificial    Type: ○ Evergreen ○ Deciduous

Notes: _____
_____

## General

Shape: ○ Vase ○ Columnar ○ Round ○ (Other) _____

Features: ○ Conical/Spire ○ Spreading ○ Upright ○ Weeping
○ (Other) _____

Branching: ○ Opposite ○ Alternate    Estimated Age: _____

Notes: _____
_____

## Needles or Leaves

Type: ○ Needle ○ Simple Broadleaf ○ Compound Broadleaf ○ Scales

Shape: ○ Cordate (heart-shaped) ○ Lanceolate (long and narrow)
○ Deltoid (triangular) ○ Obicular (round) ○ Ovate (egg-shaped)
○ Palm and Maple ○ Lobed

Structure: ○ Simple (attached to twigs or twig stems)
○ Compound (attached to single lead steam)

Notes: _____
_____

## Flowers, Fruits & Seeds

Flower Type: ○ Single Blooms ○ Clustered Blooms ○ Catkins

Fruits / Seeds: ○ Berries ○ Apples ○ Pears ○ Nuts ○ Acorns
○ Cones ○ Capsules ○ Catkins ○ (Other) _____

Notes: _____
_____

## Leaf Buds & Twigs

Bud Type: ○ Terminal (grows at tip of a shoot causing shoot to grow longer)
○ Lateral (grow along sides of a shoot causing sideways growth)

Twig Features: ○ Smooth ○ Hairy ○ Spines ○ Corky Ribs
○ (Other) _____

Notes: _____

## Bark

Texture: ○ Furrowed ○ Scaly ○ Peeling ○ Smooth ○ Shiny
○ Fissured ○ Ridges / Depressions ○ Papery ○ Warty
○ (Other) _____

Color: ○ Gray ○ Brown ○ Cinnamon ○ White ○ Silver
○ Green ○ Copper ○ (Other) _____

Notes: _____

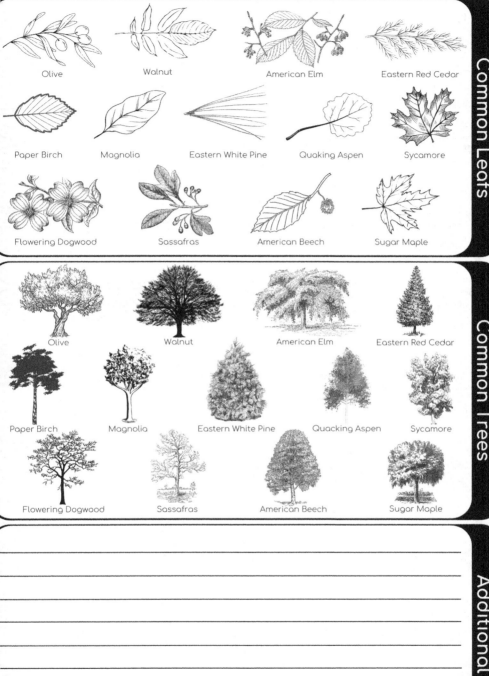

Olive

Walnut

American Elm

Eastern Red Cedar

Paper Birch

Magnolia

Eastern White Pine

Quaking Aspen

Sycamore

Flowering Dogwood

Sassafras

American Beech

Sugar Maple

Olive

Walnut

American Elm

Eastern Red Cedar

Paper Birch

Magnolia

Eastern White Pine

Quacking Aspen

Sycamore

Flowering Dogwood

Sassafras

American Beech

Sugar Maple

## Environment

Location / GPS: _____ Date _____

Season:  ◯ Spring   ◯ Summer   ◯ Fall   ◯ Winter

Surroundings:  ◯ Hedgerows  ◯ Field  ◯ Park  ◯ Woodland  ◯ Water
◯ Other _____

Setting:  ◯ Natural  ◯ Artificial   Type:  ◯ Evergreen  ◯ Deciduous

Notes: _____
_____

## General

Shape:  ◯ Vase  ◯ Columnar  ◯ Round  ◯ (Other) _____

Features:  ◯ Conical/Spire  ◯ Spreading  ◯ Upright  ◯ Weeping
◯ (Other) _____

Branching:  ◯ Opposite  ◯ Alternate   Estimated Age: _____

Notes: _____
_____

## Needles or Leaves

Type:  ◯ Needle  ◯ Simple Broadleaf  ◯ Compound Broadleaf  ◯ Scales

Shape:  ◯ Cordate (heart-shaped)  ◯ Lanceolate (long and narrow)
◯ Deltoid (triangular)  ◯ Obicular (round)  ◯ Ovate (egg-shaped)
◯ Palm and Maple  ◯ Lobed

Structure:  ◯ Simple (attached to twigs or twig stems)
◯ Compound (attached to single lead steam)

Notes: _____
_____

## Flowers, Fruits & Seeds

Flower Type:  ◯ Single Blooms  ◯ Clustered Blooms  ◯ Catkins

Fruits / Seeds:  ◯ Berries  ◯ Apples  ◯ Pears  ◯ Nuts  ◯ Acorns
◯ Cones  ◯ Capsules  ◯ Catkins  ◯ (Other) _____

Notes: _____
_____

## Leaf Buds & Twigs

Bud Type:  ◯ Terminal (grows at tip of a shoot causing shoot to grow longer)
◯ Lateral (grow along sides of a shoot causing sideways growth)

Twig Features:  ◯ Smooth  ◯ Hairy  ◯ Spines  ◯ Corky Ribs
◯ (Other) _____

Notes: _____

## Bark

Texture:  ◯ Furrowed  ◯ Scaly  ◯ Peeling  ◯ Smooth  ◯ Shiny
◯ Fissured  ◯ Ridges / Depressions  ◯ Papery  ◯ Warty
◯ (Other) _____

Color:  ◯ Gray  ◯ Brown  ◯ Cinnamon  ◯ White  ◯ Silver
◯ Green  ◯ Copper  ◯ (Other) _____

Notes: _____

Olive

Walnut

American Elm

Eastern Red Cedar

Paper Birch

Magnolia

Eastern White Pine

Quaking Aspen

Sycamore

Flowering Dogwood

Sassafras

American Beech

Sugar Maple

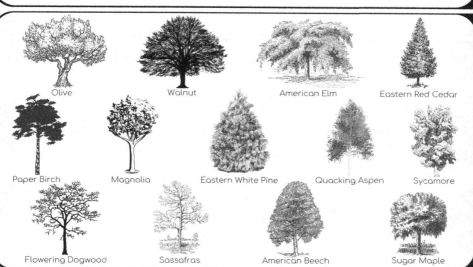

Olive

Walnut

American Elm

Eastern Red Cedar

Paper Birch

Magnolia

Eastern White Pine

Quacking Aspen

Sycamore

Flowering Dogwood

Sassafras

American Beech

Sugar Maple

## Environment

Location / GPS: _____ Date _____

Season: ○ Spring ○ Summer ○ Fall ○ Winter

Surroundings: ○ Hedgerows ○ Field ○ Park ○ Woodland ○ Water
○ Other _____

Setting: ○ Natural ○ Artificial **Type:** ○ Evergreen ○ Deciduous

Notes: _____
_____

## General

Shape: ○ Vase ○ Columnar ○ Round ○ (Other) _____

Features: ○ Conical/Spire ○ Spreading ○ Upright ○ Weeping
○ (Other) _____

Branching: ○ Opposite ○ Alternate **Estimated Age:** _____

Notes: _____
_____

## Needles or Leaves

Type: ○ Needle ○ Simple Broadleaf ○ Compound Broadleaf ○ Scales

Shape: ○ Cordate (heart-shaped) ○ Lanceolate (long and narrow)
○ Deltoid (triangular) ○ Obicular (round) ○ Ovate (egg-shaped)
○ Palm and Maple ○ Lobed

Structure: ○ Simple (attached to twigs or twig stems)
○ Compound (attached to single lead steam)

Notes: _____
_____

## Flowers, Fruits & Seeds

Flower Type: ○ Single Blooms ○ Clustered Blooms ○ Catkins

Fruits / Seeds: ○ Berries ○ Apples ○ Pears ○ Nuts ○ Acorns
○ Cones ○ Capsules ○ Catkins ○ (Other) _____

Notes: _____
_____

## Leaf Buds & Twigs

Bud Type: ○ Terminal (grows at tip of a shoot causing shoot to grow longer)
○ Lateral (grow along sides of a shoot causing sideways growth)

Twig Features: ○ Smooth ○ Hairy ○ Spines ○ Corky Ribs
○ (Other) _____

Notes: _____

## Bark

Texture: ○ Furrowed ○ Scaly ○ Peeling ○ Smooth ○ Shiny
○ Fissured ○ Ridges / Depressions ○ Papery ○ Warty
○ (Other) _____

Color: ○ Gray ○ Brown ○ Cinnamon ○ White ○ Silver
○ Green ○ Copper ○ (Other) _____

Notes: _____

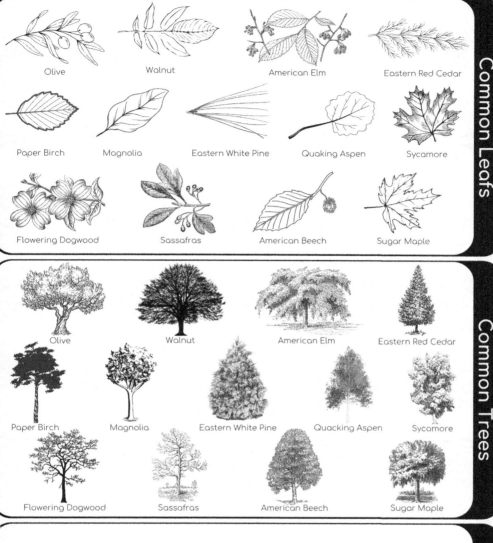

Olive

Walnut

American Elm

Eastern Red Cedar

Paper Birch

Magnolia

Eastern White Pine

Quaking Aspen

Sycamore

Flowering Dogwood

Sassafras

American Beech

Sugar Maple

Olive

Walnut

American Elm

Eastern Red Cedar

Paper Birch

Magnolia

Eastern White Pine

Quacking Aspen

Sycamore

Flowering Dogwood

Sassafras

American Beech

Sugar Maple

## Environment

Location / GPS: _____ Date _____

Season: ○ Spring ○ Summer ○ Fall ○ Winter

Surroundings: ○ Hedgerows ○ Field ○ Park ○ Woodland ○ Water
○ Other _____

Setting: ○ Natural ○ Artificial     Type: ○ Evergreen ○ Deciduous

Notes: _____
_____

## General

Shape: ○ Vase ○ Columnar ○ Round ○ (Other) _____

Features: ○ Conical/Spire ○ Spreading ○ Upright ○ Weeping
○ (Other) _____

Branching: ○ Opposite ○ Alternate     Estimated Age: _____

Notes: _____
_____

## Needles or Leaves

Type: ○ Needle ○ Simple Broadleaf ○ Compound Broadleaf ○ Scales

Shape: ○ Cordate (heart-shaped) ○ Lanceolate (long and narrow)
○ Deltoid (triangular) ○ Obicular (round) ○ Ovate (egg-shaped)
○ Palm and Maple ○ Lobed

Structure: ○ Simple (attached to twigs or twig stems)
○ Compound (attached to single lead steam)

Notes: _____
_____

## Flowers, Fruits & Seeds

Flower Type: ○ Single Blooms ○ Clustered Blooms ○ Catkins

Fruits / Seeds: ○ Berries ○ Apples ○ Pears ○ Nuts ○ Acorns
○ Cones ○ Capsules ○ Catkins ○ (Other) _____

Notes: _____
_____

## Leaf Buds & Twigs

Bud Type: ○ Terminal (grows at tip of a shoot causing shoot to grow longer)
○ Lateral (grow along sides of a shoot causing sideways growth)

Twig Features: ○ Smooth ○ Hairy ○ Spines ○ Corky Ribs
○ (Other) _____

Notes: _____

## Bark

Texture: ○ Furrowed ○ Scaly ○ Peeling ○ Smooth ○ Shiny
○ Fissured ○ Ridges / Depressions ○ Papery ○ Warty
○ (Other) _____

Color: ○ Gray ○ Brown ○ Cinnamon ○ White ○ Silver
○ Green ○ Copper ○ (Other) _____

Notes: _____

Olive

Walnut

American Elm

Eastern Red Cedar

Paper Birch

Magnolia

Eastern White Pine

Quaking Aspen

Sycamore

Flowering Dogwood

Sassafras

American Beech

Sugar Maple

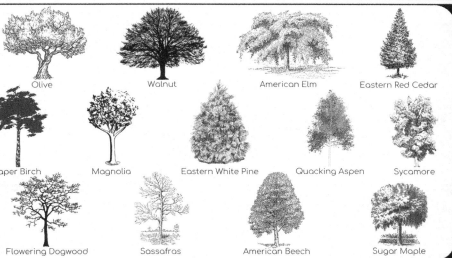

Olive

Walnut

American Elm

Eastern Red Cedar

Paper Birch

Magnolia

Eastern White Pine

Quacking Aspen

Sycamore

Flowering Dogwood

Sassafras

American Beech

Sugar Maple

## Environment

Location / GPS: _____ Date _____

Season: ⟠ Spring ⟠ Summer ⟠ Fall ⟠ Winter

Surroundings: ⟠ Hedgerows ⟠ Field ⟠ Park ⟠ Woodland ⟠ Water
⟠ Other _____

Setting: ⟠ Natural ⟠ Artificial    Type: ⟠ Evergreen ⟠ Deciduous

Notes: _____
_____

## General

Shape: ⟠ Vase ⟠ Columnar ⟠ Round ⟠ (Other) _____

Features: ⟠ Conical/Spire ⟠ Spreading ⟠ Upright ⟠ Weeping
⟠ (Other) _____

Branching: ⟠ Opposite ⟠ Alternate    Estimated Age: _____

Notes: _____
_____

## Needles or Leaves

Type: ⟠ Needle ⟠ Simple Broadleaf ⟠ Compound Broadleaf ⟠ Scales

Shape: ⟠ Cordate (heart-shaped) ⟠ Lanceolate (long and narrow)
⟠ Deltoid (triangular) ⟠ Obicular (round) ⟠ Ovate (egg-shaped)
⟠ Palm and Maple ⟠ Lobed

Structure: ⟠ Simple (attached to twigs or twig stems)
⟠ Compound (attached to single lead steam)

Notes: _____
_____

## Flowers, Fruits & Seeds

Flower Type: ⟠ Single Blooms ⟠ Clustered Blooms ⟠ Catkins

Fruits / Seeds: ⟠ Berries ⟠ Apples ⟠ Pears ⟠ Nuts ⟠ Acorns
⟠ Cones ⟠ Capsules ⟠ Catkins ⟠ (Other) _____

Notes: _____
_____

## Leaf Buds & Twigs

Bud Type: ⟠ Terminal (grows at tip of a shoot causing shoot to grow longer)
⟠ Lateral (grow along sides of a shoot causing sideways growth)

Twig Features: ⟠ Smooth ⟠ Hairy ⟠ Spines ⟠ Corky Ribs
⟠ (Other) _____

Notes: _____

## Bark

Texture: ⟠ Furrowed ⟠ Scaly ⟠ Peeling ⟠ Smooth ⟠ Shiny
⟠ Fissured ⟠ Ridges / Depressions ⟠ Papery ⟠ Warty
⟠ (Other) _____

Color: ⟠ Gray ⟠ Brown ⟠ Cinnamon ⟠ White ⟠ Silver
⟠ Green ⟠ Copper ⟠ (Other) _____

Notes: _____

Olive

Walnut

American Elm

Eastern Red Cedar

Paper Birch

Magnolia

Eastern White Pine

Quaking Aspen

Sycamore

Flowering Dogwood

Sassafras

American Beech

Sugar Maple

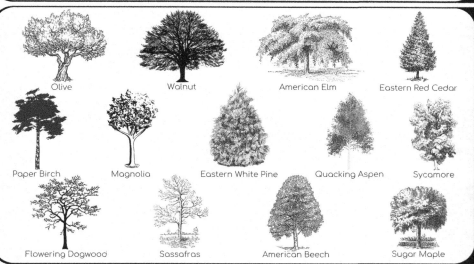

Olive

Walnut

American Elm

Eastern Red Cedar

Paper Birch

Magnolia

Eastern White Pine

Quacking Aspen

Sycamore

Flowering Dogwood

Sassafras

American Beech

Sugar Maple

## Environment

Location / GPS: _____ Date _____

Season: ○ Spring ○ Summer ○ Fall ○ Winter

Surroundings: ○ Hedgerows ○ Field ○ Park ○ Woodland ○ Water
○ Other _____

Setting: ○ Natural ○ Artificial **Type:** ○ Evergreen ○ Deciduous

Notes: _____
_____

## General

Shape: ○ Vase ○ Columnar ○ Round ○ (Other) _____

Features: ○ Conical/Spire ○ Spreading ○ Upright ○ Weeping
○ (Other) _____

Branching: ○ Opposite ○ Alternate **Estimated Age:** _____

Notes: _____
_____

## Needles or Leaves

Type: ○ Needle ○ Simple Broadleaf ○ Compound Broadleaf ○ Scales

Shape: ○ Cordate (heart-shaped) ○ Lanceolate (long and narrow)
○ Deltoid (triangular) ○ Obicular (round) ○ Ovate (egg-shaped)
○ Palm and Maple ○ Lobed

Structure: ○ Simple (attached to twigs or twig stems)
○ Compound (attached to single lead steam)

Notes: _____
_____

## Flowers, Fruits & Seeds

Flower Type: ○ Single Blooms ○ Clustered Blooms ○ Catkins

Fruits / Seeds: ○ Berries ○ Apples ○ Pears ○ Nuts ○ Acorns
○ Cones ○ Capsules ○ Catkins ○ (Other) _____

Notes: _____
_____

## Leaf Buds & Twigs

Bud Type: ○ Terminal (grows at tip of a shoot causing shoot to grow longer)
○ Lateral (grow along sides of a shoot causing sideways growth)

Twig Features: ○ Smooth ○ Hairy ○ Spines ○ Corky Ribs
○ (Other) _____

Notes: _____

## Bark

Texture: ○ Furrowed ○ Scaly ○ Peeling ○ Smooth ○ Shiny
○ Fissured ○ Ridges / Depressions ○ Papery ○ Warty
○ (Other) _____

Color: ○ Gray ○ Brown ○ Cinnamon ○ White ○ Silver
○ Green ○ Copper ○ (Other) _____

Notes: _____

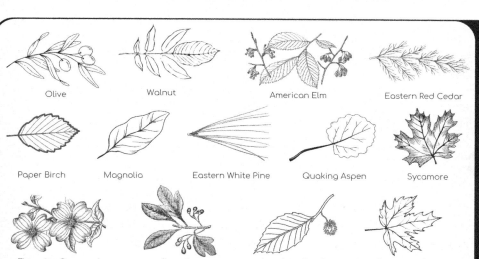

Olive

Walnut

American Elm

Eastern Red Cedar

Paper Birch

Magnolia

Eastern White Pine

Quaking Aspen

Sycamore

Flowering Dogwood

Sassafras

American Beech

Sugar Maple

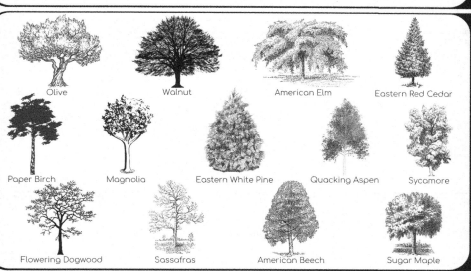

Olive

Walnut

American Elm

Eastern Red Cedar

Paper Birch

Magnolia

Eastern White Pine

Quacking Aspen

Sycamore

Flowering Dogwood

Sassafras

American Beech

Sugar Maple

## Environment

Location / GPS: _____ Date _____

Season:  ○ Spring  ○ Summer  ○ Fall  ○ Winter

Surroundings:  ○ Hedgerows  ○ Field  ○ Park  ○ Woodland  ○ Water
              ○ Other _____

Setting:  ○ Natural  ○ Artificial    Type:  ○ Evergreen  ○ Deciduous

Notes: _____
_____

## General

Shape:  ○ Vase  ○ Columnar  ○ Round  ○ (Other) _____

Features:  ○ Conical/Spire  ○ Spreading  ○ Upright  ○ Weeping
          ○ (Other) _____

Branching:  ○ Opposite  ○ Alternate    Estimated Age: _____

Notes: _____
_____

## Needles or Leaves

Type:  ○ Needle  ○ Simple Broadleaf  ○ Compound Broadleaf  ○ Scales

Shape:  ○ Cordate (heart-shaped)  ○ Lanceolate (long and narrow)
        ○ Deltoid (triangular)  ○ Obicular (round)  ○ Ovate (egg-shaped)
        ○ Palm and Maple  ○ Lobed

Structure:  ○ Simple (attached to twigs or twig stems)
            ○ Compound (attached to single lead steam)

Notes: _____
_____

## Flowers, Fruits & Seeds

Flower Type:  ○ Single Blooms  ○ Clustered Blooms  ○ Catkins

Fruits / Seeds:  ○ Berries  ○ Apples  ○ Pears  ○ Nuts  ○ Acorns
                ○ Cones  ○ Capsules  ○ Catkins  ○ (Other) _____

Notes: _____
_____

## Leaf Buds & Twigs

Bud Type:  ○ Terminal (grows at tip of a shoot causing shoot to grow longer)
          ○ Lateral (grow along sides of a shoot causing sideways growth)

Twig Features:  ○ Smooth  ○ Hairy  ○ Spines  ○ Corky Ribs
               ○ (Other) _____

Notes: _____

## Bark

Texture:  ○ Furrowed  ○ Scaly  ○ Peeling  ○ Smooth  ○ Shiny
          ○ Fissured  ○ Ridges / Depressions  ○ Papery  ○ Warty
          ○ (Other) _____

Color:  ○ Gray  ○ Brown  ○ Cinnamon  ○ White  ○ Silver
        ○ Green  ○ Copper  ○ (Other) _____

Notes: _____

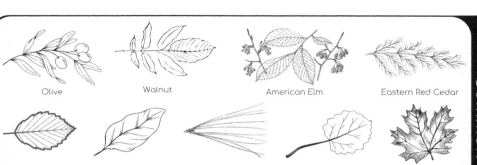

Olive  Walnut  American Elm  Eastern Red Cedar

Paper Birch  Magnolia  Eastern White Pine  Quaking Aspen  Sycamore

Flowering Dogwood  Sassafras  American Beech  Sugar Maple

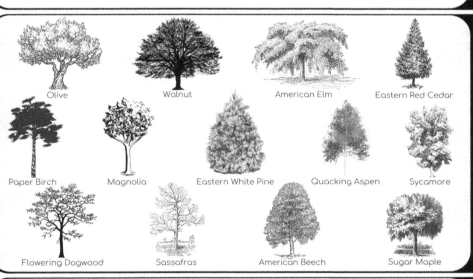

Olive  Walnut  American Elm  Eastern Red Cedar

Paper Birch  Magnolia  Eastern White Pine  Quacking Aspen  Sycamore

Flowering Dogwood  Sassafras  American Beech  Sugar Maple

## Environment

Location / GPS: _____ Date _____

Season: ○ Spring ○ Summer ○ Fall ○ Winter

Surroundings: ○ Hedgerows ○ Field ○ Park ○ Woodland ○ Water
○ Other_____

Setting: ○ Natural ○ Artificial Type: ○ Evergreen ○ Deciduous

Notes: _____
_____

## General

Shape: ○ Vase ○ Columnar ○ Round ○ (Other) _____

Features: ○ Conical/Spire ○ Spreading ○ Upright ○ Weeping
○ (Other) _____

Branching: ○ Opposite ○ Alternate Estimated Age: _____

Notes: _____
_____

## Needles or Leaves

Type: ○ Needle ○ Simple Broadleaf ○ Compound Broadleaf ○ Scales

Shape: ○ Cordate (heart-shaped) ○ Lanceolate (long and narrow)
○ Deltoid (triangular) ○ Obicular (round) ○ Ovate (egg-shaped)
○ Palm and Maple ○ Lobed

Structure: ○ Simple (attached to twigs or twig stems)
○ Compound (attached to single lead steam)

Notes: _____
_____

## Flowers, Fruits & Seeds

Flower Type: ○ Single Blooms ○ Clustered Blooms ○ Catkins

Fruits / Seeds: ○ Berries ○ Apples ○ Pears ○ Nuts ○ Acorns
○ Cones ○ Capsules ○ Catkins ○ (Other) _____

Notes: _____
_____

## Leaf Buds & Twigs

Bud Type: ○ Terminal (grows at tip of a shoot causing shoot to grow longer)
○ Lateral (grow along sides of a shoot causing sideways growth)

Twig Features: ○ Smooth ○ Hairy ○ Spines ○ Corky Ribs
○ (Other) _____

Notes: _____

## Bark

Texture: ○ Furrowed ○ Scaly ○ Peeling ○ Smooth ○ Shiny
○ Fissured ○ Ridges / Depressions ○ Papery ○ Warty
○ (Other) _____

Color: ○ Gray ○ Brown ○ Cinnamon ○ White ○ Silver
○ Green ○ Copper ○ (Other) _____

Notes: _____

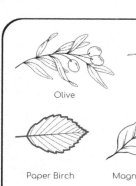

Olive

Walnut

American Elm

Eastern Red Cedar

Paper Birch

Magnolia

Eastern White Pine

Quaking Aspen

Sycamore

Flowering Dogwood

Sassafras

American Beech

Sugar Maple

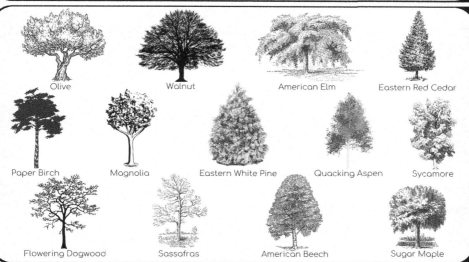

Olive

Walnut

American Elm

Eastern Red Cedar

Paper Birch

Magnolia

Eastern White Pine

Quacking Aspen

Sycamore

Flowering Dogwood

Sassafras

American Beech

Sugar Maple

## Environment

Location / GPS: _____ Date _____

Season: ○ Spring ○ Summer ○ Fall ○ Winter

Surroundings: ○ Hedgerows ○ Field ○ Park ○ Woodland ○ Water
○ Other _____

Setting: ○ Natural ○ Artificial    Type: ○ Evergreen ○ Deciduous

Notes: _____
_____

## General

Shape: ○ Vase ○ Columnar ○ Round ○ (Other) _____

Features: ○ Conical/Spire ○ Spreading ○ Upright ○ Weeping
○ (Other) _____

Branching: ○ Opposite ○ Alternate    Estimated Age: _____

Notes: _____
_____

## Needles or Leaves

Type: ○ Needle ○ Simple Broadleaf ○ Compound Broadleaf ○ Scales

Shape: ○ Cordate (heart-shaped) ○ Lanceolate (long and narrow)
○ Deltoid (triangular) ○ Obicular (round) ○ Ovate (egg-shaped)
○ Palm and Maple ○ Lobed

Structure: ○ Simple (attached to twigs or twig stems)
○ Compound (attached to single lead steam)

Notes: _____
_____

## Flowers, Fruits & Seeds

Flower Type: ○ Single Blooms ○ Clustered Blooms ○ Catkins

Fruits / Seeds: ○ Berries ○ Apples ○ Pears ○ Nuts ○ Acorns
○ Cones ○ Capsules ○ Catkins ○ (Other) _____

Notes: _____
_____

## Leaf Buds & Twigs

Bud Type: ○ Terminal (grows at tip of a shoot causing shoot to grow longer)
○ Lateral (grow along sides of a shoot causing sideways growth)

Twig Features: ○ Smooth ○ Hairy ○ Spines ○ Corky Ribs
○ (Other) _____

Notes: _____

## Bark

Texture: ○ Furrowed ○ Scaly ○ Peeling ○ Smooth ○ Shiny
○ Fissured ○ Ridges / Depressions ○ Papery ○ Warty
○ (Other) _____

Color: ○ Gray ○ Brown ○ Cinnamon ○ White ○ Silver
○ Green ○ Copper ○ (Other) _____

Notes: _____

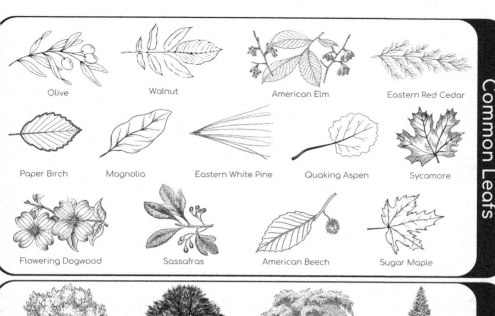

Olive    Walnut    American Elm    Eastern Red Cedar

Paper Birch    Magnolia    Eastern White Pine    Quaking Aspen    Sycamore

Flowering Dogwood    Sassafras    American Beech    Sugar Maple

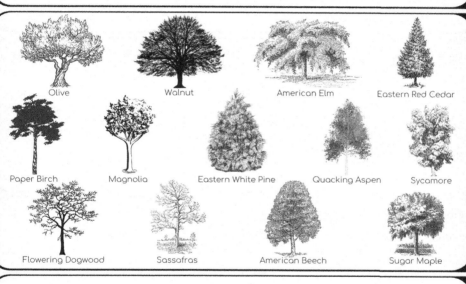

Olive    Walnut    American Elm    Eastern Red Cedar

Paper Birch    Magnolia    Eastern White Pine    Quacking Aspen    Sycamore

Flowering Dogwood    Sassafras    American Beech    Sugar Maple

## Environment

Location / GPS: _____ Date _____

Season: ○ Spring ○ Summer ○ Fall ○ Winter

Surroundings: ○ Hedgerows ○ Field ○ Park ○ Woodland ○ Water
○ Other _____

Setting: ○ Natural ○ Artificial **Type:** ○ Evergreen ○ Deciduous

Notes: _____
_____

## General

Shape: ○ Vase ○ Columnar ○ Round ○ (Other) _____

Features: ○ Conical/Spire ○ Spreading ○ Upright ○ Weeping
○ (Other) _____

Branching: ○ Opposite ○ Alternate **Estimated Age:** _____

Notes: _____
_____

## Needles or Leaves

Type: ○ Needle ○ Simple Broadleaf ○ Compound Broadleaf ○ Scales

Shape: ○ Cordate (heart-shaped) ○ Lanceolate (long and narrow)
○ Deltoid (triangular) ○ Obicular (round) ○ Ovate (egg-shaped)
○ Palm and Maple ○ Lobed

Structure: ○ Simple (attached to twigs or twig stems)
○ Compound (attached to single lead steam)

Notes: _____
_____

## Flowers, Fruits & Seeds

Flower Type: ○ Single Blooms ○ Clustered Blooms ○ Catkins

Fruits / Seeds: ○ Berries ○ Apples ○ Pears ○ Nuts ○ Acorns
○ Cones ○ Capsules ○ Catkins ○ (Other) _____

Notes: _____
_____

## Leaf Buds & Twigs

Bud Type: ○ Terminal (grows at tip of a shoot causing shoot to grow longer)
○ Lateral (grow along sides of a shoot causing sideways growth)

Twig Features: ○ Smooth ○ Hairy ○ Spines ○ Corky Ribs
○ (Other) _____

Notes: _____

## Bark

Texture: ○ Furrowed ○ Scaly ○ Peeling ○ Smooth ○ Shiny
○ Fissured ○ Ridges / Depressions ○ Papery ○ Warty
○ (Other) _____

Color: ○ Gray ○ Brown ○ Cinnamon ○ White ○ Silver
○ Green ○ Copper ○ (Other) _____

Notes: _____

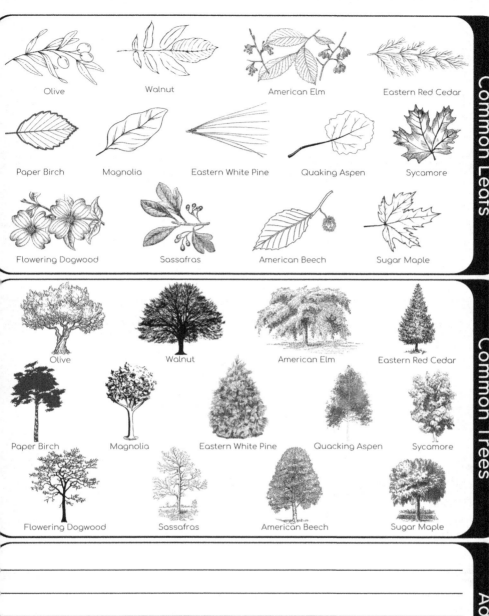

Olive
Walnut
American Elm
Eastern Red Cedar

Paper Birch
Magnolia
Eastern White Pine
Quaking Aspen
Sycamore

Flowering Dogwood
Sassafras
American Beech
Sugar Maple

Olive
Walnut
American Elm
Eastern Red Cedar

Paper Birch
Magnolia
Eastern White Pine
Quacking Aspen
Sycamore

Flowering Dogwood
Sassafras
American Beech
Sugar Maple

## Environment

Location / GPS: _____   Date _____

Season:  ◯ Spring   ◯ Summer   ◯ Fall   ◯ Winter

Surroundings:  ◯ Hedgerows   ◯ Field   ◯ Park   ◯ Woodland   ◯ Water
◯ Other_____

Setting:  ◯ Natural   ◯ Artificial      Type:  ◯ Evergreen   ◯ Deciduous

Notes: _____
_____

## General

Shape:  ◯ Vase   ◯ Columnar   ◯ Round   ◯ (Other) _____

Features:  ◯ Conical/Spire   ◯ Spreading   ◯ Upright   ◯ Weeping
◯ (Other) _____

Branching:  ◯ Opposite   ◯ Alternate      Estimated Age: _____

Notes: _____
_____

## Needles or Leaves

Type:  ◯ Needle   ◯ Simple Broadleaf   ◯ Compound Broadleaf   ◯ Scales

Shape:  ◯ Cordate (heart-shaped)   ◯ Lanceolate (long and narrow)
◯ Deltoid (triangular)   ◯ Obicular (round)   ◯ Ovate (egg-shaped)
◯ Palm and Maple   ◯ Lobed

Structure:  ◯ Simple (attached to twigs or twig stems)
◯ Compound (attached to single lead steam)

Notes: _____
_____

## Flowers, Fruits & Seeds

Flower Type:  ◯ Single Blooms   ◯ Clustered Blooms   ◯ Catkins

Fruits / Seeds:  ◯ Berries   ◯ Apples   ◯ Pears   ◯ Nuts   ◯ Acorns
◯ Cones   ◯ Capsules   ◯ Catkins   ◯ (Other) _____

Notes: _____
_____

## Leaf Buds & Twigs

Bud Type:  ◯ Terminal (grows at tip of a shoot causing shoot to grow longer)
◯ Lateral (grow along sides of a shoot causing sideways growth)

Twig Features:  ◯ Smooth   ◯ Hairy   ◯ Spines   ◯ Corky Ribs
◯ (Other) _____

Notes: _____

## Bark

Texture:  ◯ Furrowed   ◯ Scaly   ◯ Peeling   ◯ Smooth   ◯ Shiny
◯ Fissured   ◯ Ridges / Depressions   ◯ Papery   ◯ Warty
◯ (Other) _____

Color:  ◯ Gray   ◯ Brown   ◯ Cinnamon   ◯ White   ◯ Silver
◯ Green   ◯ Copper   ◯ (Other) _____

Notes: _____

Olive

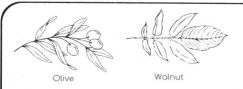
Walnut

American Elm

Eastern Red Cedar

Paper Birch

Magnolia

Eastern White Pine

Quaking Aspen

Sycamore

Flowering Dogwood

Sassafras

American Beech

Sugar Maple

Olive

Walnut

American Elm

Eastern Red Cedar

Paper Birch

Magnolia

Eastern White Pine

Quacking Aspen

Sycamore

Flowering Dogwood

Sassafras

American Beech

Sugar Maple

## Environment

Location / GPS: _____  Date _____

Season:  ○ Spring   ○ Summer   ○ Fall   ○ Winter

Surroundings:  ○ Hedgerows  ○ Field  ○ Park  ○ Woodland  ○ Water
○ Other _____

Setting:  ○ Natural   ○ Artificial      Type:  ○ Evergreen   ○ Deciduous

Notes: _____
_____

## General

Shape:  ○ Vase   ○ Columnar   ○ Round   ○ (Other) _____

Features:  ○ Conical/Spire   ○ Spreading   ○ Upright   ○ Weeping
○ (Other) _____

Branching:  ○ Opposite   ○ Alternate      Estimated Age: _____

Notes: _____
_____

## Needles or Leaves

Type:  ○ Needle   ○ Simple Broadleaf   ○ Compound Broadleaf   ○ Scales

Shape:  ○ Cordate (heart-shaped)   ○ Lanceolate (long and narrow)
○ Deltoid (triangular)  ○ Obicular (round)  ○ Ovate (egg-shaped)
○ Palm and Maple   ○ Lobed

Structure:  ○ Simple (attached to twigs or twig stems)
○ Compound (attached to single lead steam)

Notes: _____
_____

## Flowers, Fruits & Seeds

Flower Type:  ○ Single Blooms   ○ Clustered Blooms   ○ Catkins

Fruits / Seeds:  ○ Berries  ○ Apples  ○ Pears  ○ Nuts  ○ Acorns
○ Cones   ○ Capsules   ○ Catkins   ○ (Other) _____

Notes: _____
_____

## Leaf Buds & Twigs

Bud Type:  ○ Terminal (grows at tip of a shoot causing shoot to grow longer)
○ Lateral (grow along sides of a shoot causing sideways growth)

Twig Features:  ○ Smooth  ○ Hairy   ○ Spines   ○ Corky Ribs
○ (Other) _____

Notes: _____

## Bark

Texture:  ○ Furrowed  ○ Scaly  ○ Peeling  ○ Smooth  ○ Shiny
○ Fissured   ○ Ridges / Depressions   ○ Papery   ○ Warty
○ (Other) _____

Color:  ○ Gray  ○ Brown  ○ Cinnamon  ○ White  ○ Silver
○ Green   ○ Copper   ○ (Other) _____

Notes: _____

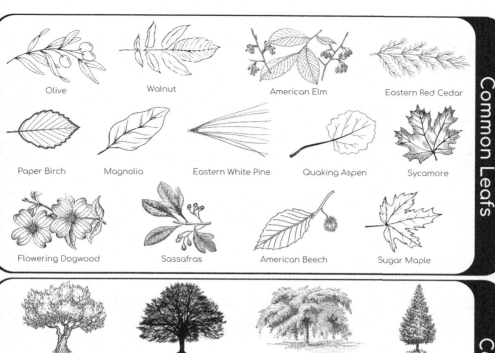

Olive

Walnut

American Elm

Eastern Red Cedar

Paper Birch

Magnolia

Eastern White Pine

Quaking Aspen

Sycamore

Flowering Dogwood

Sassafras

American Beech

Sugar Maple

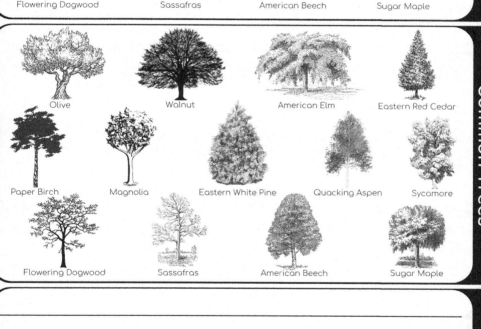

Olive

Walnut

American Elm

Eastern Red Cedar

Paper Birch

Magnolia

Eastern White Pine

Quacking Aspen

Sycamore

Flowering Dogwood

Sassafras

American Beech

Sugar Maple

## Environment

Location / GPS: _____ Date _____

Season: ○ Spring ○ Summer ○ Fall ○ Winter

Surroundings: ○ Hedgerows ○ Field ○ Park ○ Woodland ○ Water
○ Other_____

Setting: ○ Natural ○ Artificial **Type:** ○ Evergreen ○ Deciduous

Notes: _____
_____

## General

Shape: ○ Vase ○ Columnar ○ Round ○ (Other) _____

Features: ○ Conical/Spire ○ Spreading ○ Upright ○ Weeping
○ (Other) _____

Branching: ○ Opposite ○ Alternate **Estimated Age:** _____

Notes: _____
_____

## Needles or Leaves

Type: ○ Needle ○ Simple Broadleaf ○ Compound Broadleaf ○ Scales

Shape: ○ Cordate (heart-shaped) ○ Lanceolate (long and narrow)
○ Deltoid (triangular) ○ Obicular (round) ○ Ovate (egg-shaped)
○ Palm and Maple ○ Lobed

Structure: ○ Simple (attached to twigs or twig stems)
○ Compound (attached to single lead steam)

Notes: _____
_____

## Flowers, Fruits & Seeds

Flower Type: ○ Single Blooms ○ Clustered Blooms ○ Catkins

Fruits / Seeds: ○ Berries ○ Apples ○ Pears ○ Nuts ○ Acorns
○ Cones ○ Capsules ○ Catkins ○ (Other) _____

Notes: _____
_____

## Leaf Buds & Twigs

Bud Type: ○ Terminal (grows at tip of a shoot causing shoot to grow longer)
○ Lateral (grow along sides of a shoot causing sideways growth)

Twig Features: ○ Smooth ○ Hairy ○ Spines ○ Corky Ribs
○ (Other) _____

Notes: _____

## Bark

Texture: ○ Furrowed ○ Scaly ○ Peeling ○ Smooth ○ Shiny
○ Fissured ○ Ridges / Depressions ○ Papery ○ Warty
○ (Other) _____

Color: ○ Gray ○ Brown ○ Cinnamon ○ White ○ Silver
○ Green ○ Copper ○ (Other) _____

Notes: _____

Olive

Walnut

American Elm

Eastern Red Cedar

Paper Birch

Magnolia

Eastern White Pine

Quaking Aspen

Sycamore

Flowering Dogwood

Sassafras

American Beech

Sugar Maple

Olive

Walnut

American Elm

Eastern Red Cedar

Paper Birch

Magnolia

Eastern White Pine

Quacking Aspen

Sycamore

Flowering Dogwood

Sassafras

American Beech

Sugar Maple

## Environment

Location / GPS: _____  Date _____

Season:  ○ Spring  ○ Summer  ○ Fall  ○ Winter

Surroundings:  ○ Hedgerows  ○ Field  ○ Park  ○ Woodland  ○ Water
○ Other _____

Setting:  ○ Natural  ○ Artificial  **Type:**  ○ Evergreen  ○ Deciduous

Notes: _____
_____

## General

Shape:  ○ Vase  ○ Columnar  ○ Round  ○ (Other) _____

Features:  ○ Conical/Spire  ○ Spreading  ○ Upright  ○ Weeping
○ (Other) _____

Branching:  ○ Opposite  ○ Alternate  **Estimated Age:** _____

Notes: _____
_____

## Needles or Leaves

Type:  ○ Needle  ○ Simple Broadleaf  ○ Compound Broadleaf  ○ Scales

Shape:  ○ Cordate (heart-shaped)  ○ Lanceolate (long and narrow)
○ Deltoid (triangular)  ○ Obicular (round)  ○ Ovate (egg-shaped)
○ Palm and Maple  ○ Lobed

Structure:  ○ Simple (attached to twigs or twig stems)
○ Compound (attached to single lead steam)

Notes: _____
_____

## Flowers, Fruits & Seeds

Flower Type:  ○ Single Blooms  ○ Clustered Blooms  ○ Catkins

Fruits / Seeds:  ○ Berries  ○ Apples  ○ Pears  ○ Nuts  ○ Acorns
○ Cones  ○ Capsules  ○ Catkins  ○ (Other) _____

Notes: _____
_____

## Leaf Buds & Twigs

Bud Type:  ○ Terminal (grows at tip of a shoot causing shoot to grow longer)
○ Lateral (grow along sides of a shoot causing sideways growth)

Twig Features:  ○ Smooth  ○ Hairy  ○ Spines  ○ Corky Ribs
○ (Other) _____

Notes: _____

## Bark

Texture:  ○ Furrowed  ○ Scaly  ○ Peeling  ○ Smooth  ○ Shiny
○ Fissured  ○ Ridges / Depressions  ○ Papery  ○ Warty
○ (Other) _____

Color:  ○ Gray  ○ Brown  ○ Cinnamon  ○ White  ○ Silver
○ Green  ○ Copper  ○ (Other) _____

Notes: _____

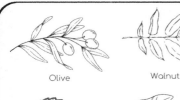
Olive

Walnut

American Elm

Eastern Red Cedar

Paper Birch

Magnolia

Eastern White Pine

Quaking Aspen

Sycamore

Flowering Dogwood

Sassafras

American Beech

Sugar Maple

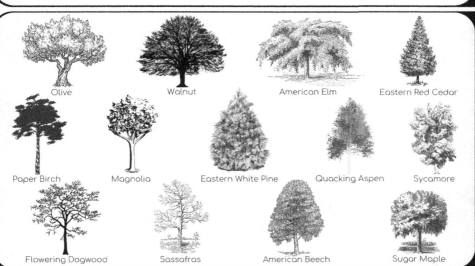

Olive

Walnut

American Elm

Eastern Red Cedar

Paper Birch

Magnolia

Eastern White Pine

Quacking Aspen

Sycamore

Flowering Dogwood

Sassafras

American Beech

Sugar Maple

## Environment

Location / GPS: _____ Date _____

Season: ⃝ Spring ⃝ Summer ⃝ Fall ⃝ Winter

Surroundings: ⃝ Hedgerows ⃝ Field ⃝ Park ⃝ Woodland ⃝ Water
⃝ Other_____

Setting: ⃝ Natural ⃝ Artificial **Type:** ⃝ Evergreen ⃝ Deciduous

Notes: _____
_____

## General

Shape: ⃝ Vase ⃝ Columnar ⃝ Round ⃝ (Other) _____

Features: ⃝ Conical/Spire ⃝ Spreading ⃝ Upright ⃝ Weeping
⃝ (Other) _____

Branching: ⃝ Opposite ⃝ Alternate **Estimated Age:** _____

Notes: _____
_____

## Needles or Leaves

Type: ⃝ Needle ⃝ Simple Broadleaf ⃝ Compound Broadleaf ⃝ Scales

Shape: ⃝ Cordate (heart-shaped) ⃝ Lanceolate (long and narrow)
⃝ Deltoid (triangular) ⃝ Obicular (round) ⃝ Ovate (egg-shaped)
⃝ Palm and Maple ⃝ Lobed

Structure: ⃝ Simple (attached to twigs or twig stems)
⃝ Compound (attached to single lead steam)

Notes: _____
_____

## Flowers, Fruits & Seeds

Flower Type: ⃝ Single Blooms ⃝ Clustered Blooms ⃝ Catkins

Fruits / Seeds: ⃝ Berries ⃝ Apples ⃝ Pears ⃝ Nuts ⃝ Acorns
⃝ Cones ⃝ Capsules ⃝ Catkins ⃝ (Other) _____

Notes: _____
_____

## Leaf Buds & Twigs

Bud Type: ⃝ Terminal (grows at tip of a shoot causing shoot to grow longer)
⃝ Lateral (grow along sides of a shoot causing sideways growth)

Twig Features: ⃝ Smooth ⃝ Hairy ⃝ Spines ⃝ Corky Ribs
⃝ (Other) _____

Notes: _____

## Bark

Texture: ⃝ Furrowed ⃝ Scaly ⃝ Peeling ⃝ Smooth ⃝ Shiny
⃝ Fissured ⃝ Ridges / Depressions ⃝ Papery ⃝ Warty
⃝ (Other) _____

Color: ⃝ Gray ⃝ Brown ⃝ Cinnamon ⃝ White ⃝ Silver
⃝ Green ⃝ Copper ⃝ (Other) _____

Notes: _____

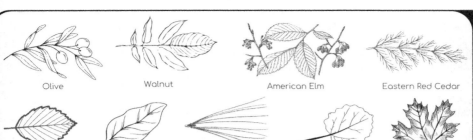

Olive

Walnut

American Elm

Eastern Red Cedar

Paper Birch

Magnolia

Eastern White Pine

Quaking Aspen

Sycamore

Flowering Dogwood

Sassafras

American Beech

Sugar Maple

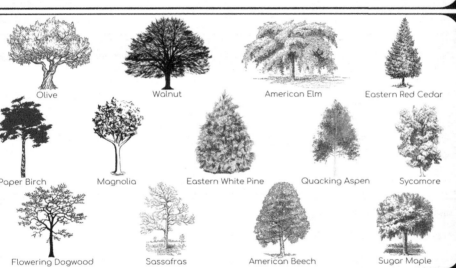

Olive

Walnut

American Elm

Eastern Red Cedar

Paper Birch

Magnolia

Eastern White Pine

Quacking Aspen

Sycamore

Flowering Dogwood

Sassafras

American Beech

Sugar Maple

## Environment

Location / GPS: _____  Date _____

Season:  ○ Spring  ○ Summer  ○ Fall  ○ Winter

Surroundings:  ○ Hedgerows  ○ Field  ○ Park  ○ Woodland  ○ Water
○ Other _____

Setting:  ○ Natural  ○ Artificial  **Type:** ○ Evergreen  ○ Deciduous

Notes: _____
_____

## General

Shape:  ○ Vase  ○ Columnar  ○ Round  ○ (Other) _____

Features:  ○ Conical/Spire  ○ Spreading  ○ Upright  ○ Weeping
○ (Other) _____

Branching:  ○ Opposite  ○ Alternate  **Estimated Age:** _____

Notes: _____
_____

## Needles or Leaves

Type:  ○ Needle  ○ Simple Broadleaf  ○ Compound Broadleaf  ○ Scales

Shape:  ○ Cordate (heart-shaped)  ○ Lanceolate (long and narrow)
○ Deltoid (triangular)  ○ Obicular (round)  ○ Ovate (egg-shaped)
○ Palm and Maple  ○ Lobed

Structure:  ○ Simple (attached to twigs or twig stems)
○ Compound (attached to single lead steam)

Notes: _____
_____

## Flowers, Fruits & Seeds

Flower Type:  ○ Single Blooms  ○ Clustered Blooms  ○ Catkins

Fruits / Seeds:  ○ Berries  ○ Apples  ○ Pears  ○ Nuts  ○ Acorns
○ Cones  ○ Capsules  ○ Catkins  ○ (Other) _____

Notes: _____
_____

## Leaf Buds & Twigs

Bud Type:  ○ Terminal (grows at tip of a shoot causing shoot to grow longer)
○ Lateral (grow along sides of a shoot causing sideways growth)

Twig Features:  ○ Smooth  ○ Hairy  ○ Spines  ○ Corky Ribs
○ (Other) _____

Notes: _____

## Bark

Texture:  ○ Furrowed  ○ Scaly  ○ Peeling  ○ Smooth  ○ Shiny
○ Fissured  ○ Ridges / Depressions  ○ Papery  ○ Warty
○ (Other) _____

Color:  ○ Gray  ○ Brown  ○ Cinnamon  ○ White  ○ Silver
○ Green  ○ Copper  ○ (Other) _____

Notes: _____

## Common Leafs

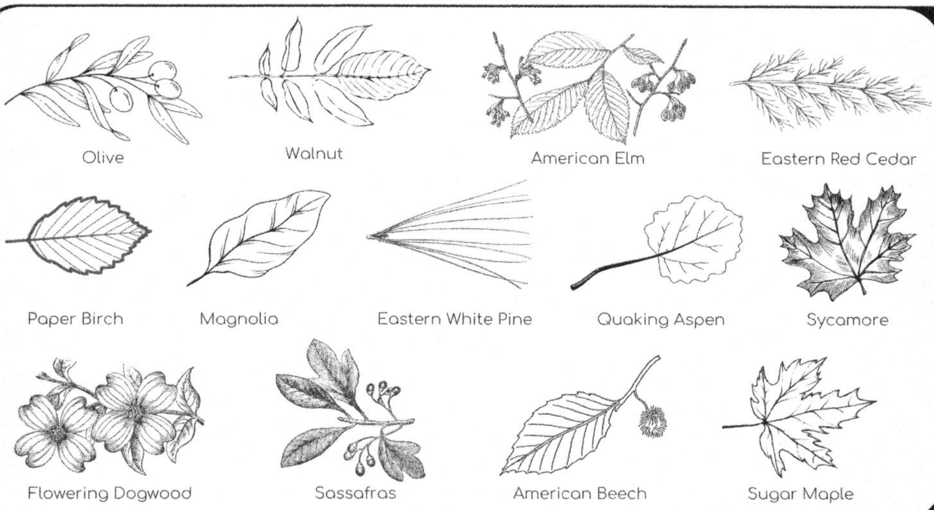

Olive
Walnut
American Elm
Eastern Red Cedar
Paper Birch
Magnolia
Eastern White Pine
Quaking Aspen
Sycamore
Flowering Dogwood
Sassafras
American Beech
Sugar Maple


## Common Trees

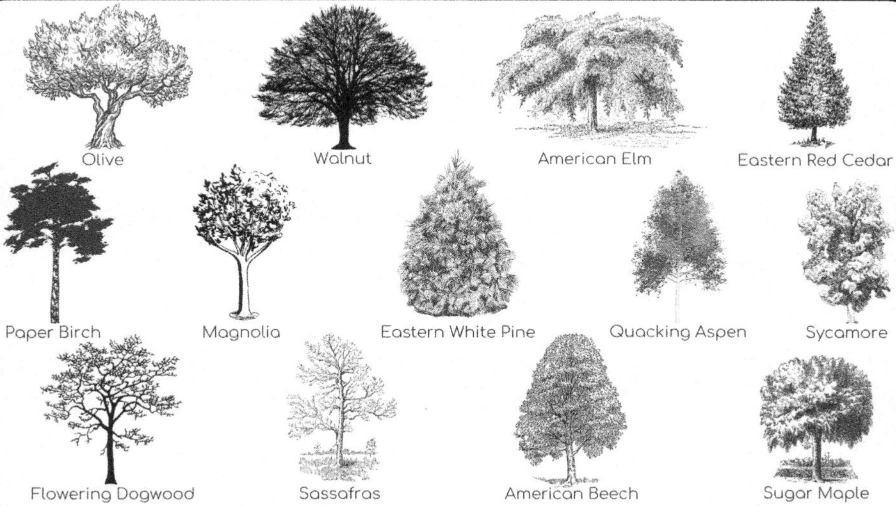

Olive
Walnut
American Elm
Eastern Red Cedar
Paper Birch
Magnolia
Eastern White Pine
Quacking Aspen
Sycamore
Flowering Dogwood
Sassafras
American Beech
Sugar Maple


## Additional Notes

## Environment

Location / GPS: _____ Date _____

Season: ○ Spring    ○ Summer    ○ Fall    ○ Winter

Surroundings: ○ Hedgerows    ○ Field    ○ Park    ○ Woodland    ○ Water
○ Other_____

Setting: ○ Natural    ○ Artificial    Type: ○ Evergreen    ○ Deciduous

Notes: _____
_____

## General

Shape: ○ Vase    ○ Columnar    ○ Round    ○ (Other) _____

Features: ○ Conical/Spire    ○ Spreading    ○ Upright    ○ Weeping
○ (Other) _____

Branching: ○ Opposite    ○ Alternate    Estimated Age: _____

Notes: _____
_____

## Needles or Leaves

Type: ○ Needle    ○ Simple Broadleaf    ○ Compound Broadleaf    ○ Scales

Shape: ○ Cordate (heart-shaped)    ○ Lanceolate (long and narrow)
○ Deltoid (triangular)    ○ Obicular (round)    ○ Ovate (egg-shaped)
○ Palm and Maple    ○ Lobed

Structure: ○ Simple (attached to twigs or twig stems)
○ Compound (attached to single lead steam)

Notes: _____
_____

## Flowers, Fruits & Seeds

Flower Type: ○ Single Blooms    ○ Clustered Blooms    ○ Catkins

Fruits / Seeds: ○ Berries    ○ Apples    ○ Pears    ○ Nuts    ○ Acorns
○ Cones    ○ Capsules    ○ Catkins    ○ (Other) _____

Notes: _____
_____

## Leaf Buds & Twigs

Bud Type: ○ Terminal (grows at tip of a shoot causing shoot to grow longer)
○ Lateral (grow along sides of a shoot causing sideways growth)

Twig Features: ○ Smooth    ○ Hairy    ○ Spines    ○ Corky Ribs
○ (Other) _____

Notes: _____

## Bark

Texture: ○ Furrowed    ○ Scaly    ○ Peeling    ○ Smooth    ○ Shiny
○ Fissured    ○ Ridges / Depressions    ○ Papery    ○ Warty
○ (Other) _____

Color: ○ Gray    ○ Brown    ○ Cinnamon    ○ White    ○ Silver
○ Green    ○ Copper    ○ (Other) _____

Notes: _____

## Common Leafs

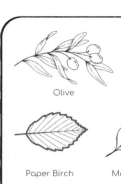
Olive

Walnut

American Elm

Eastern Red Cedar

Paper Birch

Magnolia

Eastern White Pine

Quaking Aspen

Sycamore

Flowering Dogwood

Sassafras

American Beech

Sugar Maple

## Common Trees

Olive

Walnut

American Elm

Eastern Red Cedar

Paper Birch

Magnolia

Eastern White Pine

Quacking Aspen

Sycamore

Flowering Dogwood

Sassafras

American Beech

Sugar Maple

## Additional Notes

## Environment

Location / GPS: _____ Date _____

Season: ○ Spring ○ Summer ○ Fall ○ Winter

Surroundings: ○ Hedgerows ○ Field ○ Park ○ Woodland ○ Water
○ Other _____

Setting: ○ Natural ○ Artificial **Type:** ○ Evergreen ○ Deciduous

Notes: _____
_____

## General

Shape: ○ Vase ○ Columnar ○ Round ○ (Other) _____

Features: ○ Conical/Spire ○ Spreading ○ Upright ○ Weeping
○ (Other) _____

Branching: ○ Opposite ○ Alternate **Estimated Age:** _____

Notes: _____
_____

## Needles or Leaves

Type: ○ Needle ○ Simple Broadleaf ○ Compound Broadleaf ○ Scales

Shape: ○ Cordate (heart-shaped) ○ Lanceolate (long and narrow)
○ Deltoid (triangular) ○ Obicular (round) ○ Ovate (egg-shaped)
○ Palm and Maple ○ Lobed

Structure: ○ Simple (attached to twigs or twig stems)
○ Compound (attached to single lead steam)

Notes: _____
_____

## Flowers, Fruits & Seeds

Flower Type: ○ Single Blooms ○ Clustered Blooms ○ Catkins

Fruits / Seeds: ○ Berries ○ Apples ○ Pears ○ Nuts ○ Acorns
○ Cones ○ Capsules ○ Catkins ○ (Other) _____

Notes: _____
_____

## Leaf Buds & Twigs

Bud Type: ○ Terminal (grows at tip of a shoot causing shoot to grow longer)
○ Lateral (grow along sides of a shoot causing sideways growth)

Twig Features: ○ Smooth ○ Hairy ○ Spines ○ Corky Ribs
○ (Other) _____

Notes: _____

## Bark

Texture: ○ Furrowed ○ Scaly ○ Peeling ○ Smooth ○ Shiny
○ Fissured ○ Ridges / Depressions ○ Papery ○ Warty
○ (Other) _____

Color: ○ Gray ○ Brown ○ Cinnamon ○ White ○ Silver
○ Green ○ Copper ○ (Other) _____

Notes: _____

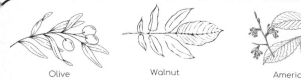

Olive    Walnut    American Elm    Eastern Red Cedar

Paper Birch    Magnolia    Eastern White Pine    Quaking Aspen    Sycamore

Flowering Dogwood    Sassafras    American Beech    Sugar Maple

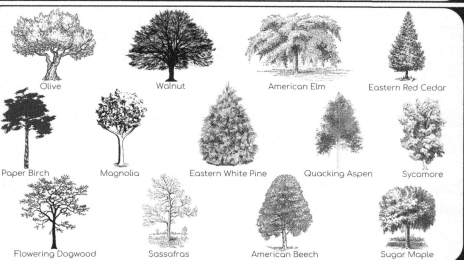

Olive    Walnut    American Elm    Eastern Red Cedar

Paper Birch    Magnolia    Eastern White Pine    Quacking Aspen    Sycamore

Flowering Dogwood    Sassafras    American Beech    Sugar Maple

## Environment

Location / GPS: _____ Date _____

Season: ○ Spring  ○ Summer  ○ Fall  ○ Winter

Surroundings: ○ Hedgerows  ○ Field  ○ Park  ○ Woodland  ○ Water
○ Other_____

Setting: ○ Natural  ○ Artificial  **Type:** ○ Evergreen  ○ Deciduous

Notes: _____
_____

## General

Shape: ○ Vase  ○ Columnar  ○ Round  ○ (Other) _____

Features: ○ Conical/Spire  ○ Spreading  ○ Upright  ○ Weeping
○ (Other) _____

Branching: ○ Opposite  ○ Alternate  **Estimated Age:** _____

Notes: _____
_____

## Needles or Leaves

Type: ○ Needle  ○ Simple Broadleaf  ○ Compound Broadleaf  ○ Scales

Shape: ○ Cordate (heart-shaped)  ○ Lanceolate (long and narrow)
○ Deltoid (triangular)  ○ Obicular (round)  ○ Ovate (egg-shaped)
○ Palm and Maple  ○ Lobed

Structure: ○ Simple (attached to twigs or twig stems)
○ Compound (attached to single lead steam)

Notes: _____
_____

## Flowers, Fruits & Seeds

Flower Type: ○ Single Blooms  ○ Clustered Blooms  ○ Catkins

Fruits / Seeds: ○ Berries  ○ Apples  ○ Pears  ○ Nuts  ○ Acorns
○ Cones  ○ Capsules  ○ Catkins  ○ (Other) _____

Notes: _____
_____

## Leaf Buds & Twigs

Bud Type: ○ Terminal (grows at tip of a shoot causing shoot to grow longer)
○ Lateral (grow along sides of a shoot causing sideways growth)

Twig Features: ○ Smooth  ○ Hairy  ○ Spines  ○ Corky Ribs
○ (Other) _____

Notes: _____

## Bark

Texture: ○ Furrowed  ○ Scaly  ○ Peeling  ○ Smooth  ○ Shiny
○ Fissured  ○ Ridges / Depressions  ○ Papery  ○ Warty
○ (Other) _____

Color: ○ Gray  ○ Brown  ○ Cinnamon  ○ White  ○ Silver
○ Green  ○ Copper  ○ (Other) _____

Notes: _____

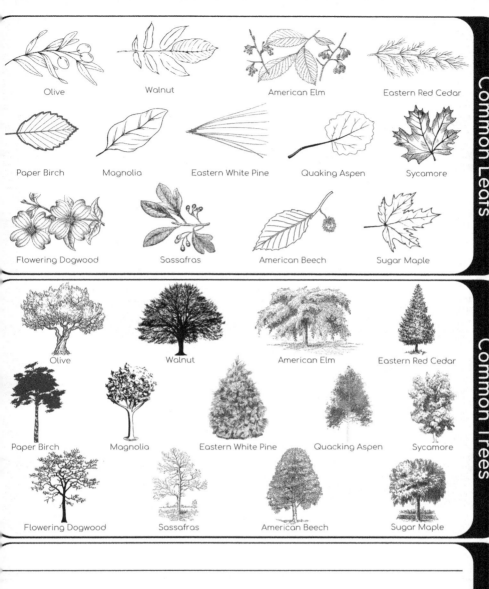

Olive

Walnut

American Elm

Eastern Red Cedar

Paper Birch

Magnolia

Eastern White Pine

Quaking Aspen

Sycamore

Flowering Dogwood

Sassafras

American Beech

Sugar Maple

Olive

Walnut

American Elm

Eastern Red Cedar

Paper Birch

Magnolia

Eastern White Pine

Quacking Aspen

Sycamore

Flowering Dogwood

Sassafras

American Beech

Sugar Maple

## Environment

Location / GPS: _____   Date _____

Season: ○ Spring  ○ Summer  ○ Fall  ○ Winter

Surroundings: ○ Hedgerows  ○ Field  ○ Park  ○ Woodland  ○ Water
○ Other _____

Setting: ○ Natural  ○ Artificial   Type: ○ Evergreen  ○ Deciduous

Notes: _____
_____

## General

Shape: ○ Vase  ○ Columnar  ○ Round  ○ (Other) _____

Features: ○ Conical/Spire  ○ Spreading  ○ Upright  ○ Weeping
○ (Other) _____

Branching: ○ Opposite  ○ Alternate   Estimated Age: _____

Notes: _____
_____
_____

## Needles or Leaves

Type: ○ Needle  ○ Simple Broadleaf  ○ Compound Broadleaf  ○ Scales

Shape: ○ Cordate (heart-shaped)  ○ Lanceolate (long and narrow)
○ Deltoid (triangular)  ○ Obicular (round)  ○ Ovate (egg-shaped)
○ Palm and Maple  ○ Lobed

Structure: ○ Simple (attached to twigs or twig stems)
○ Compound (attached to single lead steam)

Notes: _____
_____

## Flowers, Fruits & Seeds

Flower Type: ○ Single Blooms  ○ Clustered Blooms  ○ Catkins

Fruits / Seeds: ○ Berries  ○ Apples  ○ Pears  ○ Nuts  ○ Acorns
○ Cones  ○ Capsules  ○ Catkins  ○ (Other) _____

Notes: _____
_____

## Leaf Buds & Twigs

Bud Type: ○ Terminal (grows at tip of a shoot causing shoot to grow longer)
○ Lateral (grow along sides of a shoot causing sideways growth)

Twig Features: ○ Smooth  ○ Hairy  ○ Spines  ○ Corky Ribs
○ (Other) _____

Notes: _____

## Bark

Texture: ○ Furrowed  ○ Scaly  ○ Peeling  ○ Smooth  ○ Shiny
○ Fissured  ○ Ridges / Depressions  ○ Papery  ○ Warty
○ (Other) _____

Color: ○ Gray  ○ Brown  ○ Cinnamon  ○ White  ○ Silver
○ Green  ○ Copper  ○ (Other) _____

Notes: _____

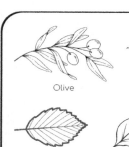
Olive

Walnut

American Elm

Eastern Red Cedar

Paper Birch

Magnolia

Eastern White Pine

Quaking Aspen

Sycamore

Flowering Dogwood

Sassafras

American Beech

Sugar Maple

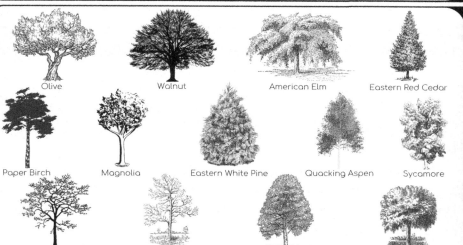

Olive

Walnut

American Elm

Eastern Red Cedar

Paper Birch

Magnolia

Eastern White Pine

Quacking Aspen

Sycamore

Flowering Dogwood

Sassafras

American Beech

Sugar Maple

## Environment

Location / GPS: _____  Date _____

Season: ○ Spring  ○ Summer  ○ Fall  ○ Winter

Surroundings: ○ Hedgerows  ○ Field  ○ Park  ○ Woodland  ○ Water
○ Other _____

Setting: ○ Natural  ○ Artificial     Type: ○ Evergreen  ○ Deciduous

Notes: _____
_____

## General

Shape: ○ Vase  ○ Columnar  ○ Round  ○ (Other) _____

Features: ○ Conical/Spire  ○ Spreading  ○ Upright  ○ Weeping
○ (Other) _____

Branching: ○ Opposite  ○ Alternate     Estimated Age: _____

Notes: _____
_____

## Needles or Leaves

Type: ○ Needle  ○ Simple Broadleaf  ○ Compound Broadleaf  ○ Scales

Shape: ○ Cordate (heart-shaped)  ○ Lanceolate (long and narrow)
○ Deltoid (triangular)  ○ Obicular (round)  ○ Ovate (egg-shaped)
○ Palm and Maple  ○ Lobed

Structure: ○ Simple (attached to twigs or twig stems)
○ Compound (attached to single lead steam)

Notes: _____
_____

## Flowers, Fruits & Seeds

Flower Type: ○ Single Blooms  ○ Clustered Blooms  ○ Catkins

Fruits / Seeds: ○ Berries  ○ Apples  ○ Pears  ○ Nuts  ○ Acorns
○ Cones  ○ Capsules  ○ Catkins  ○ (Other) _____

Notes: _____
_____

## Leaf Buds & Twigs

Bud Type: ○ Terminal (grows at tip of a shoot causing shoot to grow longer)
○ Lateral (grow along sides of a shoot causing sideways growth)

Twig Features: ○ Smooth  ○ Hairy  ○ Spines  ○ Corky Ribs
○ (Other) _____

Notes: _____

## Bark

Texture: ○ Furrowed  ○ Scaly  ○ Peeling  ○ Smooth  ○ Shiny
○ Fissured  ○ Ridges / Depressions  ○ Papery  ○ Warty
○ (Other) _____

Color: ○ Gray  ○ Brown  ○ Cinnamon  ○ White  ○ Silver
○ Green  ○ Copper  ○ (Other) _____

Notes: _____

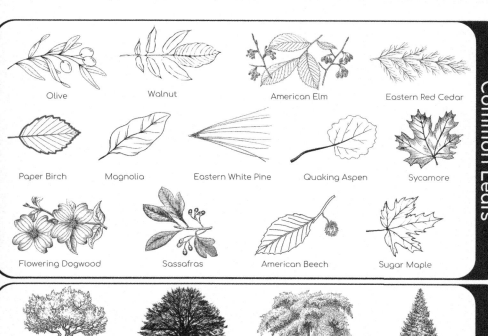

Olive    Walnut    American Elm    Eastern Red Cedar

Paper Birch    Magnolia    Eastern White Pine    Quaking Aspen    Sycamore

Flowering Dogwood    Sassafras    American Beech    Sugar Maple

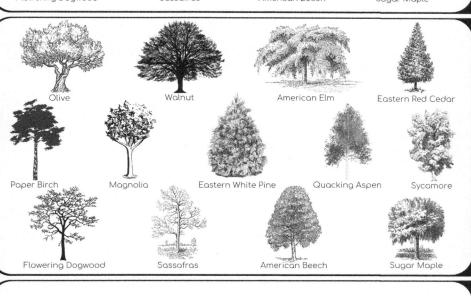

Olive    Walnut    American Elm    Eastern Red Cedar

Paper Birch    Magnolia    Eastern White Pine    Quacking Aspen    Sycamore

Flowering Dogwood    Sassafras    American Beech    Sugar Maple

Made in the USA
Monee, IL
14 June 2022